Models for Writing

Teacher's Book 3

Chris Buckton

Anne Sanderson

Series editor: Leonie Bennett

GINN

Author Team Chris Buckton
               Anne Sanderson
Series editor: Leonie Bennett

               Bill Ball (Scottish 5–14 Guidelines)
               Robert Hunter (Northern Ireland Curriculum)
               Beverley Parker and Steve Yates (ICT)

Ginn
Linacre House, Jordan Hill, Oxford, OX2 8DP
a division of Reed Educational and Professional Publishing Ltd
www.ginn.co.uk

Ginn is a registered trademark of Reed Educational and Professional Publishing Ltd

© Reed Educational and Professional Publishing Ltd 2000

ISBN 0602 296811

04 03 02 01
10 9 8 7 6 5 4 3 2

Designed and produced by Gecko Ltd, Bicester, Oxon
Cover design by Gecko Ltd, Bicester, Oxon
Printed in the UK by Ashford Colour Press, Hampshire.

Contents

Introduction

Welcome to *Models for Writing*, the first complete programme to deliver Shared, Guided and Extended writing at Key Stage 2 in line with the requirements of the National Literacy Strategy framework. This programme links writing inside the Literacy Hour with extended writing outside the hour in a structured way. *Models for Writing* offers thorough coverage of the NLS writing objectives (*see matching chart on page 10*).

It also covers the requirements of the Scottish Guidelines on English Language 5 – 14 (1991), and the Northern Ireland Curriculum (1996) (*see correlation charts on pages 11 and 12*).

Improving Children's Writing

Models for Writing will help you to improve your pupils' writing across the ability range, bringing as many pupils as possible up to level 4 by the end of year 6.

It helps to improve writing through:

- stimulating model texts that interest and excite pupils
- modelled writing sessions which provide children with a clear structure
- differentiated activities and extended writing
- guided writing sessions that focus on both text and sentence level work.

Differentiation

Differentiation is offered in group and guided activities in the **Pupil's Book**. The activities are flagged with the following symbols:

1 Work for **lower attainers**, often supported by a photocopy master.

2 Work for the whole class. **Lower attainers** are often supported by a photocopy master such as a writing frame.

3 Work for **higher attainers**.

The lesson plans for each unit (*see pages 38–97*) offer specific guidance on how to work with different attaining groups during Guided writing.

Assessment

Models for Writing helps you to assess children's writing and judge how their skills are developing. You will find guidelines on assessment and annotated samples of children's writing at different levels on pages 22–31.

SAT Preparation

Suggestions for which units to use to practise writing under timed conditions are offered on pages 35–37.

Information and Communication Technology

Models for Writing includes a comprehensive section of ICT activities for each unit (*see pages 102–108*).

In the lesson plans, the **ICT** symbol indicates when an ICT activity could be used for that unit, and cross-references you to the appropriate page in the ICT section.

Structure/Components

Models for Writing has a simple structure which links Shared and Guided writing in the Literacy Hour with extended writing outside of the Hour.

Each Year of *Models for Writing* has:

Pupil's Book containing model texts, guided and supported activities, and extended writing.

Pupil's Book

Teacher's Book offering lesson plans for each unit, curriculum matching charts, assessment guidance, and ICT activities.

Teacher's Book

Overhead Transparencies of model texts and writing frames for whole class teaching.

Colour Overhead Transparancies

Photocopy Masters for differentiation and homework.

Photocopy Masters

How to use *Models for Writing*

When to Use *Models for Writing*

Each unit is designed around two lessons, with an additional extended writing session. You can use **Models for Writing** alongside any other literacy programme by slotting the two lessons into your planning. Alternatively, you could choose to spend more time on a particular unit or theme (*see 'Linked Units' below*) and extend the lessons over a whole week. Each unit focuses on a single writing objective, making it easy for you to see where they fit into your teaching, and making **Models for Writing** an extremely flexible programme.

How each unit works

Models for Writing is made up of 30 units. In each unit you will find:

LESSON ONE: MODEL TEXT

- The first lesson focuses on the study of a short model text from the **Pupil's Book**. (The text provides the model for the next lesson's writing.) Where annotation of the text is required, it is also offered on an OHT.

- Differentiated group activities are offered through the **Pupil's Book** and the **Photocopy Masters**.

LESSON TWO: WRITING

- *Shared Writing* – Shared or modelled writing based on the model text. Writing or planning frames are offered as OHTs where needed.

- *Guided, Group and Independent Writing* – Differentiated group and guided activities. Guidance is given on which group to work with during the guided writing session.

EXTENDED WRITING

- Each unit ends with a suggested extended writing activity, to be completed outside of the lesson.

LINKED UNITS

- Some units are linked by topic or theme, or explore a particular skill at different levels. Opportunites for linking units are highlighted in the Planning Suggestion section of the lesson plan.

How to use *Models for Writing*

A *Models for Writing* Unit

LESSON ONE

LESSON TWO

Model Text

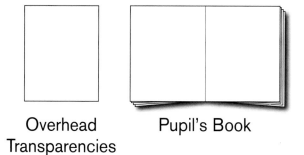

Overhead Transparencies

Pupil's Book

Shared Writing

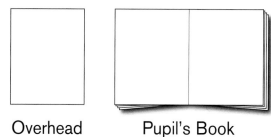

Overhead Transparencies

Pupil's Book

Group Activities

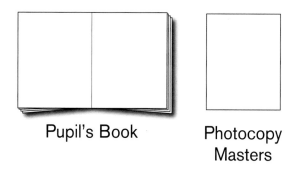

Pupil's Book

Photocopy Masters

Guided/Supported Writing

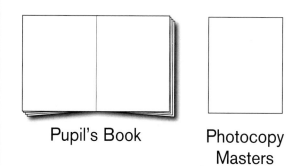

Pupil's Book

Photocopy Masters

Homework

Photocopy Masters

Extended Writing

Pupil's Book

How to use this Teacher's Book

main writing objective of unit with reference to NLS framework

unit number

unit heading

text type/ genre

word and sentence level objectives

OHTs and PCMs needed are highlighted

suggestions for exploring the model text

differentiated group activities for the whole class

suggested homework activity

1 Talking to Jamila Gavin
● STORY IDEAS

MAIN WRITING OBJECTIVE
● **To generate ideas by brainstorming, word association, etc.**   3.1 T9

Word and sentence level objective
● To investigate a range of devices for presenting texts.   3.1 S9

LESSON ONE

MODEL TEXT

● Explain the lesson objective: *to find out how an author gets ideas for her stories.*

● Jamila Gavin was born in India. Many of her ideas for stories come from things that happened to her when she was little.

● Read the interview aloud, displaying the star chart and discussing it as you read the opening paragraph. Briefly discuss where pupils get their ideas for stories. Do they use their own lives?

● Why does Jamila Gavin ask so many questions when she is thinking of story ideas? *to find out lots of detail about the characters, to work out how they will behave*

● Why do pupils think her top tip is to 'write about things that really mean something to you'? *you'll know and understand it better*

● Discuss the stages of a story. Ask pupils to pick out the important words and phrases in paragraph 3. *beginning, problem, next, comes out right*

● Look at the questions on the star chart. Ask pupils to imagine the questions are about themselves. Encourage them to think of as many different answers as possible and note all the suggestions down. This process is called **brainstorming**. It helps you to collect as many ideas as you can before you write a story.

● Do pupils know the difference between FACT and FICTION? Their answers to the questions are FACTS because they are real. Authors often start with facts like these, but go on to write about imaginary people and events. This is FICTION.

Word and sentence level work
Ask pupils to explain what a star chart is in their own words. Why is this a useful way to make notes when brainstorming ideas?

Group activities: differentiation
All pupils make their own ME star chart using **PCM 1**.
Higher attainers could add some more questions of their own.

Plenary
Share star charts. What questions have pupils added? Discuss how one question leads to another and how this helps you to explore ideas.

YOU WILL NEED
● **Pupil's Book** page 4
● **OHT 1** – Star Chart
● Flipchart
● **PCM 1** – ME star chart

ICT For activities linked to this lesson see **PAGE 102**

HOMEWORK
Pupils should take home their star charts and decide which of the ideas would make the best story. Encourage them to carry on asking questions and brainstorming ideas for the story on the back of the sheet.

38

8

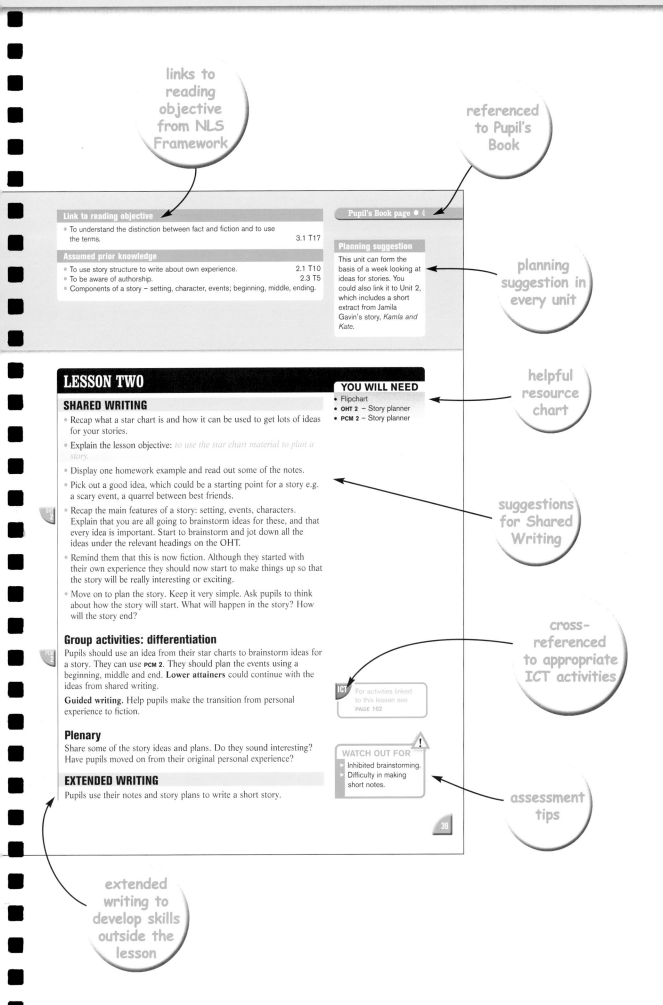

links to reading objective from NLS Framework

referenced to Pupil's Book

Pupil's Book page ● 4

Link to reading objective

- To understand the distinction between fact and fiction and to use the terms.   3.1 T17

Assumed prior knowledge

- To use story structure to write about own experience.   2.1 T10
- To be aware of authorship.   2.3 T5
- Components of a story – setting, character, events; beginning, middle, ending.

Planning suggestion

This unit can form the basis of a week looking at ideas for stories. You could also link it to Unit 2, which includes a short extract from Jamila Gavin's story, *Kamla and Kate.*

planning suggestion in every unit

LESSON TWO

SHARED WRITING

- Recap what a star chart is and how it can be used to get lots of ideas for your stories.
- Explain the lesson objective: *to use the star chart material to plan a story.*
- Display one homework example and read out some of the notes.
- Pick out a good idea, which could be a starting point for a story e.g. a scary event, a quarrel between best friends.
- Recap the main features of a story: setting, events, characters. Explain that you are all going to brainstorm ideas for these, and that every idea is important. Start to brainstorm and jot down all the ideas under the relevant headings on the OHT.
- Remind them that this is now fiction. Although they started with their own experience they should now start to make things up so that the story will be really interesting or exciting.
- Move on to plan the story. Keep it very simple. Ask pupils to think about how the story will start. What will happen in the story? How will the story end?

Group activities: differentiation

Pupils should use an idea from their star charts to brainstorm ideas for a story. They can use **PCM 2**. They should plan the events using a beginning, middle and end. **Lower attainers** could continue with the ideas from shared writing.

Guided writing. Help pupils make the transition from personal experience to fiction.

Plenary

Share some of the story ideas and plans. Do they sound interesting? Have pupils moved on from their original personal experience?

EXTENDED WRITING

Pupils use their notes and story plans to write a short story.

YOU WILL NEED
- Flipchart
- **OHT 2** – Story planner
- **PCM 2** – Story planner

helpful resource chart

suggestions for Shared Writing

ICT For activities linked to this lesson see **PAGE 102**

cross-referenced to appropriate ICT activities

! WATCH OUT FOR
▸ Inhibited brainstorming.
▸ Difficulty in making short notes.

assessment tips

39

extended writing to develop skills outside the lesson

NLS Writing Objectives Matching Chart

MAIN WRITING OBJECTIVE

Term 1 – Fiction
- T9 — To generate ideas by brainstorming, word association etc.
- T10 — To use reading as a model to write own passages of dialogue.
- T11 — To develop the use of settings in stories.
- T12 — To collect sentences/phrases for story openings and endings.
- T13 — To collect suitable words and phrases in order to write poems.
- T14 — To invent calligrams and a range of shape poems.
- T15 — To write simple playscripts based on own reading and oral work.
- T16 — To begin to organise stories into paragraphs.

Term 1 – Non-fiction
- T22 — To make a simple record of information from texts read.
- T23 — To write simple non-chronological reports from known information.

Term 2 – Fiction
- T6 — To plan main points as a structure for story writing; to discuss different methods of planning.
- T7 — To describe and sequence key incidents e.g. by mapping.
- T8 — To write portraits of characters.
- T9 — To write a story plan for own myth, fable or traditional tale.
- T10 — To write alternative sequels to traditional tales.
- T11 — To write new or extended verses for performance poetry based on models.

Term 2 – Non-fiction
- T16 — To write instructions, e.g. rules using a range of organisational devices.
- T17 — To make clear notes through: identifying the purpose for which particular notes will be used; exploring ways of writing ideas in, shortened forms, e.g. notes, lists, headlines; making use of simple formats to capture key points.

Term 3 – Fiction
- T10 — To plot a sequence of episodes modelled on a known story.
- T11 — To write openings to stories or chapters.
- T12 — To write a first person account.
- T13 — To write extended stories based on a plan.
- T14 — To write book reviews for a specified audience.
- T15 — To write poetry that uses sound to create effects.

Term 3 – Non-fiction
- T20 — To write letters to authors about books.
- T21 — To use IT to bring to a published form.
- T22 — To experiment with recounting the same event in a variety of ways.
- T23 — To organise letters in to simple paragraphs.
- T24 — To make alphabetically ordered texts.
- T26 — To summarise in writing the content of a passage and the main point.

Unit	1F T9	1F T10	1F T11	1F T12	1F T13	1F T14	1F T15	1F T16	1NF T22	1NF T23	2F T6	2F T7	2F T8	2F T9	2F T10	2F T11	2NF T16	2NF T17	3F T10	3F T11	3F T12	3F T13	3F T14	3F T15	3NF T20	3NF T21	3NF T22	3NF T23	3NF T24	3NF T26
1 Talking to Jamila Gavin	✓																													
2 Familiar Places			✓																											
3 Cat Speak		✓																												
4 Harry's Party							✓																							
5 Ace Dragon Ltd								✓																						
6 People and Places										✓																				
7 Rhythm Machine					✓																									
8 Frogs and Toads									✓																					
9 Like and Hate						✓																								
10 Once Upon a Time ... the End				✓																										
11 Who? What? Where?											✓																			
12 A Poor Widow's Son													✓																	
13 Memo to Me																		✓												
14 Jack's Journey												✓																		
15 Hamsters must not ...																	✓													
16 Too Much Searching														✓																
17 Mighty Mountain															✓															
18 How to ...																	✓													
19 Getting to the Point																		✓												
20 The Hairy Toe																✓														
21 Sea World																														✓
22 Market Street Mystery																											✓			
23 Diary of a Killer Cat																					✓									
24 May we recommend																							✓							
25 Dear Author																									✓			✓		
26 Flood! 1																			✓			✓								
27 Flood! 2																				✓		✓								
28 The Sound Collector																								✓						
29 A to Z Book																										✓			✓	

Scottish 5–14 Curriculum Guideline Levels

STRAND	LEVEL A	UNITS	LEVEL B	UNITS
Functional Writing	**Write briefly for a simple practical purpose.** • Teacher will assist in observing, selecting, ordering and scribing. • Discussion before, during and after activities. • Report orally to teacher and others. • Sequence through drawings and flow charts.	3 22 8 25 11 26 13 14 15 18 19	**Write briefly in an appropriate form for a variety of practical purposes.** • Letters and reports of events that they have been involved in. • Simple notes to assist in sequencing events. • Consider audience – pupils, parents etc. • Write real letters to public figures, to seek information. • Teacher to introduce different styles of writing for different purposes.	21 29 30
Personal Writing	**Write briefly about a personal experience.** • Initially through discussion supported by teacher. • After drawing, discuss detail as basis for story. • Teacher will help decide main points. • First stories may be single sentence. • Use of word banks etc. • Move on to several sentences.	6 7 9 28	**Write briefly and in an appropriate sequence about a personal experience, giving an indication of feelings, using adequate vocabulary.** • Sequence developed through pictures in order and a sentence written for each. • In discussion singly and in groups reflect on stories and reshape them. • Use other writing as models. • With teacher assistance begin to articulate feelings. • Use of concept keyboard.	30
Imaginative Writing	**Write a brief imaginative story.** • A character may be used as the focus for imaginary events. • Story tapes, TV, class books can be starting point. • Model good stories and sequencing using class novels.	1 2 4 5 10 12	**Write a brief imaginative story or poem or dialogue with discernible organisation and using adequate vocabulary.** • Using a model and by discussing appropriate vocabulary teachers help pupils draft what they wish to say. • Discuss in groups first draft. • Teacher to introduce plot, character, setting, dialogue etc through class stories. • Model poetry through a wide variety of poems – rhyme less important than rhythm, content and vocabulary.	4 16 17 20 23 24 27 28 30
Punctuation and Structure	**In the writing tasks listed, use capital letters and full stops correctly in more than one sentence.** • Use pupils' own reading books to model sentence structure. • Children can use these conventions in their own work. • Provide meaningful contexts for such work.	2 19 3 20 5 22 7 25 8 26 10	**In the writing tasks listed use capital letters and full stops correctly in more than one sentence and use common linking words – and then, but, so, that.** • Use capital letters and full stops to establish meaning through teacher support. • Link sentences with common and familiar words.	4 30 21 23 24 27 28
Knowledge About Language	**Go over words, sounds, capital letters and full stops to enable children to use in above strands. These should be introduced through contexts rather than stand alone.**	1 16 6 17 11 12 13 14 15	**Show that they know understand and can use at least the following terms – letter, word, capital letter, full stop, sentence, planning, drafting, editing.** • Teacher to model all of these in reading etc and pupils should be aware of them in their own work. • Pupils will use planning, drafting and editing throughout the writing process.	9 29 30

The strands for Spelling and Handwriting and Presentation would be covered by the teacher differentiating according to each pupil's ability.

Models for Writing and the Northern Ireland Curriculum

UNIT	LEVEL	Opportunities are provided for:
1	3	
2	3	**WRITING**
3	3	• Modelled writing
4	3	• Shared writing
5	3	• Writing for a variety of purposes
6	3	• Planning, drafting, revising and publishing • Collaborative work
7	3	• Extending vocabulary • Beginning to use appropriate form, showing a sense of structure and
8	3	organisation
9	3	• Discussing features of layout • Using some supporting detail to improve meaning
10	3	• Presenting ideas and information logically
11	3	• Developing knowledge of and using basic punctuation with accuracy • Responding to reading
12	3	• Teaching note making
13	3	• Using problem solving to analyse texts • Experimenting with rhymes, rhythms, verbal play and poetic forms
14	3	• Differentiated responses
15	3	**READING**
16	3	• Reading aloud
17	3	• Beginning to use a range of vocabulary when referring to texts • Composing, reading and sharing their own books of stories and poems
18	3	• Modelling writing on forms encountered in reading
19	3	• Recognising the main points • Recognising a sequence of events
20	3	• Beginning to use evidence in the text to support their views
21	3	• Talking about the features of written language
22	3	• Reading for a variety of purposes
23	3	**TALKING AND LISTENING**
24	3	• Engaging in formal and informal discussion • Asking and answering questions
25	3	• Giving instructions, information and explanations
26	3	• Talking about their work to other pupils and the teacher • Expressing thoughts, feelings and opinions
27	3	• Listening to and saying poems
28	3	• Listening to and responding to guidance and instructions given by the teacher • Describing and talking about real and imagined experiences
29	3	• Sharing and co-operating in pairs
30	3	• Discussing features of language

About Shared Writing

In Shared Writing, you, the 'expert writer', model the writing process. Pupils should contribute ideas, calling on their experience of exploring the model text, and you develop them further.

Before Writing

Talk with the pupils about:

- the text type and its features ●
- the purpose and audience ●
- the structure, and how best to order the events or information
- the layout – length, illustration and final presentation
- possible ways of planning – brainstorming, story boards, writing ● frames etc.

> What do we know about texts like these?

> Who are we writing for?

> How can we organise our ideas?

During Shared Writing

- where appropriate, display the annotated model text so the class can refer to it
- explain exactly what you like or do not like about the ideas the pupils offer
- demonstrate how to share ideas and work collaboratively
- 'think aloud' as you write so that pupils understand how to ● consider different options
- demonstrate how writers work at each stage of composition
- show pupils how to apply the conventions of written English – focus on specific aspects of punctuation or spelling
- demonstrate how to revise the writing by re-reading and making changes
- keep the writing short.

> I'm making this into a longer sentence by adding extra detail.

After Writing

Show pupils how to:

- talk about their writing; introduce the vocabulary they will need
- edit and redraft their work, perhaps moving larger chunks of text ● as well as adding and deleting words and phrases
- make the link between reading and writing, considering their work as a reader would – What does it make you feel? What is left out ● or not clear?
- proof-read, checking for sense as well as spelling and punctuation errors
- prepare for final presentation.

> Let's add an adjective to describe what he looks like. How should we describe him?

> Does this sound right? Is it better if we take out these words?

REMEMBER

Do

- share the lesson objective with the pupils
- emphasise purpose and audience
- refer back to the model text
- direct and control the Shared Writing
- encourage pupils to contribute at their own level
- build on pupils' suggestions
- write with pupils whenever possible
- 'think aloud' as you are writing
- encourage pupils to revise as they write
- teach self-help techniques
- expect pupils to proof-read and edit their work

Don't

- offer unfocused praise
- be afraid to make specific criticisms
- try to correct every aspect of their writing

About Guided Writing

Guided Writing is about providing support for children during the writing process.

For Guided Writing, children should be in small groups according to writing ability. You may teach specific skills, or dip in and out of writing with the pupils, discussing as you go. Providing support while children are working is especially important.

Offer guidance throughout the writing process. On pages 16–19 you will find Prompt Charts to help you guide pupils through each stage of composition.

Before Writing

Help pupils to prepare by:

- reviewing the task

Who are we writing for?

- collecting ideas – maybe by brainstorming or spider webbing
- talking about how to organise the material – choosing key ideas, grouping them, putting them in the best order, working out how to link them

How shall we group all our ideas?

- jotting down words and phrases that might be useful
- checking for gaps in their plan.

During Writing

Join the group when they are already writing. Observe for a while, then:

- find out how it is going and identify any problems

What could we add to give us more detail?

- focus on specific elements of composition, just a few sentences at a time
- remind pupils of the model text and the work done in Shared Writing
- help to develop ideas and build confidence

That's a really good connective because...

- use appropriate terminology.

After Writing

Respond to pupils' work by:

What are we looking for in this text?

- finding out what the writers were trying to achieve
- reviewing the task and recapping the features of the text type
- asking writers to read out sections they are pleased with
- giving precise, positive feedback which lets writers know what effect their writing has had on a reader

I liked the bit when...

- asking writers to identify the parts which need development
- encouraging suggestions for improvement.

Teaching sequence for Guided Writing when planning written work

STEPS	TYPICAL CUES
Review	• What do we know about writing texts like this? • What is the job in hand? • How shall we go about it?
Gather ideas	• What do we want to say? • What ideas do we have?
Marshal the material (select – shape – sequence)	• Which ideas shall we use? • How can we group ideas together? • What order should we put them in? • How can we link the ideas together?
Gather support	• What details can we add? • How can we explain or expand? • What evidence can we give? • What words and expressions come to mind?
Rehearse	• Does it look right? • What are the gaps? • How could we start? • How can it be improved?

Teaching sequence for Guided Writing when pupils are drafting

STEPS	TYPICAL CUES
Review	• What's the task in hand? • What do we know already? • What are the main features of this kind of text? • How did the author in yesterday's Shared Reading tackle this?
Cue in	• How might you start? • Let me start you off . . . • Let's try starting with action this time.
Try it	• Identification • Exploration/generalisation • Addition/deletion/substitution • Praise/building confidence • Assessment • Use of terminology/reflection • Extension/development • Drawing writing into talk
Recapitulate	• What worked? • What helped? • What can we use again?

Teaching sequence for Guided Writing when responding to written work

STEPS	TYPICAL CUES
Recapitulate	• What are we looking for in this piece of writing? • What are the main features of this kind of text?
Read and reward	• What I liked about this was . . . • That makes me wonder . . . • I noticed . . . • Where are the best moments?
Compare and generalise	• Who else tried it that way? • What other ways have been used? • Which of these worked well? • Which tends to work best?
Isolate weakness	• Where are the false notes? • Why does it not quite work? • Which is the hardest part to get right? • What could be improved?
Support improvement	• How could you deal with the problem? • Could we say . . .? • You could try . . . • Start like this . . . • Try writing that part again . . .

Teaching activities: intervening in the writing process

1 Identification/Selection of important features	What I noticed/liked about this was . . . because . . .
2 Addition Deletion Substitution	What can we add? What can we leave out/get rid of? What else can we put in there to make it better?
3 Exploration/Generalisation	The reason why . . . It's useful to know that . . . What tends to work best is . . . because . . . The rule/pattern for this is . . . When else does this happen?
4 Praise/Building confidence	I really like the way you . . . because . . . I really like . . . because . . . That works well because . . .
5 Assessment Assessing strengths, weaknesses Correction	Which parts work best? Why does it not quite work? Which is the hardest part to get right?
6 Use of terminology/Reflection	I really like the term you chose because . . . Which term could you use here?
7 Extension/Development	Could we use, say . . .? You could try . . . You can carry on by . . .
8 Drawing writing into talking	Tell me how you would write . . . So you think that . . . What do you think about . . .? Say a little more about . . .

Independent and Extended Writing

Independent Writing

Independent writing activities flow directly from Shared or Guided Writing. In independent group activities, pupils are still supported by working collaboratively and by using writing frames. **Writing frames can be a powerful support for writers but they can also become a straightjacket. It is very important to show pupils how to adapt them and how to generate their own.** Support also comes from exploring the model text, the preparatory work completed for homework and the Shared Writing session.

Models for Writing also provides **Prompt Charts** which list the main features of each text type or writing process, and these can be displayed for pupils to refer to. (The **Prompt Charts** are located at the back of the **Photocopy Masters** folder.)

Extended Writing

The suggestions for extended writing in *Models for Writing* encourage pupils to carry on with their writing outside the Literacy Hour; to discuss and revise their work; to take their work to presentation standard and, where appropriate, to publish it using ICT. The lesson plans that accompany each unit offer suggestions for how you might integrate the units and the extended writing activities into your weekly planning.

Models for Writing emphasises that writing for different purposes requires different approaches. A shopping list or a quick note will not require redrafting, but a brochure about the school, or a web site, might take several sessions to complete.

Pair and Collaborative Writing: Response Partners

Models for Writing offers pupils ample opportunity to talk about their work and to help each other by giving feedback, as well as times when they can write in near silence. Their feedback will be most effective if they are given guidance and practice in reading each other's work and giving advice on it. Encourage them to act as response partners on a regular basis.

At first their comments may be superficial. They need to learn to:

- find out what the writer is trying to do
- pay attention to content
- identify which features to comment on
- balance positive and negative comments
- be constructive.

On pages 32–34 you will find **Self-Assessment** sheets to support this process. Discuss and model the process in Shared and Guided Writing.

Assessing Children's Writing:
how to improve your pupils' work

Knowing it is good or bad is not good enough!

To reach literacy targets, we need to know *precisely* what pupils need to improve upon. What are the features in pupil X's writing that make him so fluent? What *exactly* are the difficulties that pupil Y is having which may prevent her reaching level 4 by the end of Key Stage 2? If you can diagnose the symptoms you are on the way to finding a cure. Through careful assessment and specific feedback, you and your pupils will find out what they can do already and what they need to do next. On the basis of this you can plan future tasks to take their learning forward. The most helpful assessments focus on a few specific features. Too much information can be overwhelming and de-motivating.

If the learning objective is clear and precise then assessment is easy. Much of the assessment occurs with the pupil during writing, particularly in guided group work. Talking together helps you to find out what the writer is trying to do and what difficulties they are encountering.

Pupils can also get feedback for themselves. Make sure they know the purpose of every writing task and the criteria for assessing it. Show them how to assess their own writing against the criteria and how to work effectively with a response partner.

Prompt Charts

To check whether the piece of writing has the appropriate structure and features for its 'genre' or 'text type', use the Prompt Charts at the back of the **Photocopy Masters** folder.

You can also give these charts to pupils to help them remember the criteria, and structure their writing accordingly.

Self-Assessment

Ask pupils to use **Photocopy Master** A (*see page 32*) to assist their work with a response partner. They can also use **Photocopy Master** B (*see page 33*) for support with their editing, and **Photocopy Master** C (*see page 34*) to assess their own work.

Help them to develop the habit of reflecting on their own writing. If they are involved in setting their own targets they will be much more motivated to achieve them.

Questions to Consider

Purpose and audience

- Is the form of the writing suitable for its purpose?
- Is the writer aware of the reader?
- Does the writing engage the reader's interest?

Structure and organisation

- How effective are the opening and ending?
- How well does the writer organise ideas?
- Does the structure reflect the features of the text type?
- Is sentence construction varied?
- Are sentences and paragraphs joined with a variety of connectives?

Grammar and style

- Is the writing grammatically correct?
- Is punctuation used correctly?
- Are verb tenses consistent?
- Is there unnecessary repetition?
- Does the writing flow?
- Is it coherent?
- Is the vocabulary well chosen?

Presentation

- Is handwriting or word processing clear and suitable for the purpose?
- Is the presentation appropriate?

Spelling

- Is spelling usually accurate?
- Does spelling show knowledge of word derivation, common patterns, and prefixes/suffixes?
- Are guesses plausible?

Fiction: The Key
Achievements: Level 3
Purpose and audience:
NLS 3.1 T11 To develop the use of settings in own stories.

Summary

The task set was to write an adventure story for reading to another class. The final draft was to be made into a book.
Peter's story 'speaks' to the audience effectively and carries the reader along.

Structure and Organisation

- A fluent piece which is well constructed with confident scene setting.

- Good ending – the last sentence ties up the narrative in a satisfying way.

- Clear organisation.

- Good grasp of narrative conventions.

Grammar and Style

- Variety of sentence construction.

- Grammatically correct; flows well through the use of connectives ('It wasn't that long till . . .')

- Detail adds interest ('jingling noise').

- Realistic dialogue.

- Punctuation accurate – some use of commas to indicate grammatical boundaries within sentences.

- Apostrophes for contractions.

- No speech marks or paragraphing.

Spelling

- Most high frequency words correctly spelt. Occasional errors but phonetically plausible.

- Good grasp of doubling consonants.

What next?

- Basic conventions of speech punctuation and paragraphing. Work on expanding the climax and resolution of the story.

THE KEY

One day me and David were in the country side on our own. We were ment to be looking at trees but David said we should go exploring. We were on a pavement by a long road. We will walk a bit longer till we find something strange. It wasn't that long till we heard a jingling noise at our feet. I looked down and there was a key. Look at this I said. Wow, he said. I wonder who dropped it there I asked. Lets look every where for a look which fits it. We looked on trees and on pavements. On one tree David spotted a lock. I tried it and it fitted just right. We opened it and a door swung open. There were stairs going down. David lead the way down them. Right at the bottom was a little room. There was a box in the middle of the room. We were over excited, because we had never even been underground

befor. I open it then I said. David opened the box. Inside were 2 gold coins and many silver coins. They all had the face of queen Victoria on them. We shared them out. It was a long way home but at last we made it. We put the coins in a secret place. So that was our storys, a secret that nobody knew.

I am writing my story for heven year olds.

PETER

Fiction: Poem with repeating phrases
Achievements: Level 2 with some level 3 elements
Purpose and audience:
NLS 3.1 T12 To collect suitable words and phrases in order to write poems; design simple patterns with words, use repetitive phrases.

Summary

The poem was written after a poetry workshop, using prescribed structure from a model. The purpose was to make a class anthology to send to the poet.

Structure and Organisation

- Understood and replicated the question/answer pattern, including line layout.
- Has chosen vivid memory for first verse; second verse less specific.

Grammar and Style

- No question marks.
- A missing full stop.
- No title.

Spelling

- Accurate – used word book to correct errors in first draft.
- Some capital letters incorrectly used (Football, Was)
- 'p' descender error.

What next?

- Work on powerful verb alternatives for 'played'. Try question and answer ballads, haiku and riddles to extend descriptive vocabulary.
- Try inventing own pattern.

Where's the Walkers crisps
that I threw about in my pram
When I was 1
Eaten

Where's my Football
that I Played With
When I Was 4
Burst.

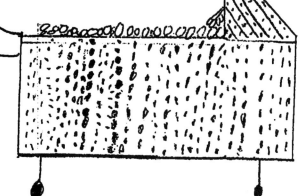

Non-fiction: Victorian Diary
Achievements: Level 3
Purpose and audience:
NLS 3.2 T7   To describe and sequence key incidents.
NLS 3.2 T17 To make clear notes through exploring ways of
writing in shortened form.

Summary

After watching a video about Victorians, the task set was to summarise a maid's day, and then turn it into a fictional diary, including the maid's feelings.
The pupil has a reasonably secure grasp of the task, but is not clear about conveying the character's feelings. This lack of characterisation limits interest.

Structure and Organisation

- Can handle and use historical data successfully.

- Consistent control of diary format.

- Logical sequence, realistic time frame.

Grammar and Style

- Sentences abbreviated to suit diary style. Understands note-making.

- Accurate punctuation.

- A few slips into present tense towards end ('blow', 'go').

- Uncertainty over irregular verbs ('sweeped').

- A bit pedestrian – hasn't conveyed character and there is a lack of lively vocabulary.

Spelling

- Mainly correct – errors in unfamiliar words phonetically plausible.

- Knows -ed ending but not yet always correctly applied.

- Some capitalisation errors mid-sentence ('and Dressed').

What next?

- The task was clearly too ambitious – included using historical data, diary format AND characterisation. It would be better to concentrate on feelings as a separate piece of writing, e.g. maid's letter home.

- Work on irregular verbs.

Monday 6th November   A Day in the Life of a Servant

6.30. am   got up, brushed my hair

7. am   stripped the beds and layed the table.

7.30 am   Served breakfast and washed up.

8. am   polished the silver and sweeped the kichen floor.

8.30 am   Sweeped the living room floor, fed the cat and cleaned the stairs.

9.30 a.m.   Sweeped under all the rugs and dusted all the walls

10. am   I cleaned all the bedrooms and hung all the washing out to dry.

11. a.m   layed the table and polished the silver

11.30 am   served the lunch and then cleaned the windows.

12 o'clock mid-day   I cleaned the toilet and then bront the dry washing in.

1pm   fed the cat its lunch and made the bed up for bed time

2.30 p.m   I cleaned the furniter and dusted all the cabinits.

4.30. p.m   Dusted all the shelves and cuburds and layed the table

5.30 pm   Served supper and washed-up the dishes.

6.30 pm   dusted all the china and cleaned the master's and mistress'es shoes.

7.30 p.m   gave the cat its food and swept the carpets and rugs

8.30 p.m   I took water up to the master and mistress in bed and cleaned the kitchen floor.

9pm   blow out all the candles and go to bed.

Non-fiction: American Indians
Achievements: Level 3
Purpose and audience:
NLS 3.1 T22 To make simple non-chronological reports from texts read.

Summary

This report was written as a contribution to a group topic book, with the rest of the class as the audience. The children brainstormed headings together and used reference books to research information. The piece shows some sense of audience (e.g. explaining what an eagle is) but other terms not explained sufficiently, e.g. tribe names. Some interesting detail.

Structure and Organisation

- Clearly organised into short paragraphs.
- Content logically related to headings.
- Sentence construction fairly simple although includes some connectives ('...went hunting while...').
- Uses own words – no sign of wholesale copying.
- Has picked out key facts.

Grammar and Style

- Consistent use of capital letters and full stops for sentence punctuation.
- Erratic tenses – moves between past and present.
- Reasonably coherent.

Spelling

- Plausible attempts at unfamilar words showing knowledge of spelling conventions('necklesses', 'streached').
- Confusion over there/their.

What next?

- Increase accuracy in verb tenses. Further explanation of detail (e.g. expand 'streached beavers and ferrets'). Encourage use of drawings/diagrams.

Monday 15th March

How life was in a North American camp

Food

Native North Americans use to eat eagle Eagle is an animal that is similar to a black bird. They kill it by a bow and arrow. Then they cooked the eagle on a really hot fire.

Work

The men went hunting for food like buffalo while the ladies wash the clothes The men teach there sons how to hunt. When the men come back with there food they cook it. The women make clothes like seminole and Tlingit

Clothes

Women and men made moccasins by Sewing buffalo skin together with grass.

Women and men used to wear Navajo and seminole and tlingit.

Fun

The children Sometimes played hockey. The men played lacrosse children also played wars little brother.

Homes

Some Indians lived in earth lodges. Earth lodges was were not good homes to live in. Wig wams were built by the Algonquin great lakes. Chickees were built near lakes.

Animals

North Americans Streached beavers and ferrets North Americans skinned the buffalo and used the bones to make necklesses.

Working with a response partner

Read your work aloud.

Is it interesting/enjoyable?

Is anything not clear? List below.

-
-
-

Is anything missing? List below.

-
-
-

Can you suggest:

- alternative words or expressions?

- a better beginning or ending?

Is it too long or too short?

Can anything be cut? If so, what?

Has the writer done what he or she was asked to do?

Editing checklist

Remember to check:	checked ✓
Are there enough details to help the reader?	☐
Have you used capital letters and punctuation?	☐
Is speech set out correctly?	☐
Do all verbs and nouns agree?	☐
Are all spellings correct?	☐
Are there any repeated phrases or unneccessary words that you can take out?	☐

Self-assessment

Title of writing: _____

What was the task? _____

_____

_____

How difficult was it? (Circle the score out of 10)

    1   2   3   4   5   6   7   8   9   10

How happy are you with it? (Circle the score out of 10)

    1   2   3   4   5   6   7   8   9   10

What do you think you have done well?

_____

_____

What didn't work?

_____

_____

What did your response partner say about it?

_____

_____

Do you agree?

_____

What is your new target?

_____

_____

Models for Writing and Year 3 SATs preparation

The six pieces of writing below can be set under timed conditions. It is a good idea to set one piece of timed writing every half term. Give the pupils 15 minutes to plan the task and 45 minutes to complete their writing.

Unit 2 Familiar Places

TASK: Write a story set in a place you know well.
(This could be linked to ideas covered in Shared Writing.) You should use interesting details to paint a vivid picture of the setting.

Assessment Criteria

Purpose and audience
- Is the form of writing suitable for the purpose?
- Does the story engage the readers' interest?

Structure and organisation
- Is the setting clearly established?
- Does the story have a strong opening paragraph?
- Is the story coherent, with a clear beginning, middle and end?

Grammar and style
- Are sentences correctly indicated by full stops, capital letters, question marks?
- Does it include descriptive words and phrases?
- Does the writing use precise details?
- Does the story flow well through the use of connectives?

Unit 6 People and Places

TASK: Write a report about a person or a place you know well.

Assessment Criteria

Purpose and audience
- Is the form of writing suitable for the purpose and audience?

Structure and organisation
- Is there a short introduction?
- Are related facts grouped into paragraphs?

Grammar and style
- Are sentences correctly indicated by full stops and capital letters?
- Is the writing mainly present tense?
- Is the report coherent?

Unit 15 Hamsters must not ...

TASK: Write some rules for children at your school and in the playground.

Assessment Criteria

Purpose and audience
- Is the form of writing suitable for the purpose and audience?

Structure and organisation
- Are the rules concise?
- Are the rules organised into bullet points or numbers?
- Has thought been given to layout and use of illustrations?

Grammar and style
- Is it written in the second person?
- Are verbs used at the beginning of sentences?
- Does it adopt an appropriate tone of voice?

Unit 18 How to ...

TASK: Write a set of instructions for an alien on how to survive on earth.

Assessment Criteria

Purpose and audience
- Is the form of writing suitable for the purpose?
- Is the writer aware of the needs of the reader?

Structure and organisation
- Are the instructions organised into numbered steps?
- Is the layout appropriate?
- Are the instructions clear?

Grammar and style
- Are verbs used at the beginning of sentences?
- Is the vocabulary appropriate?
- Are the sentences correctly punctuated?
- Are the instructions presented in a clear, coherent style?

Unit 22 The Market Street Mystery

TASK: Write a newspaper report.
(This is linked to the subject matter covered in Shared Writing.)

Assessment Criteria

Purpose and audience

- Is the form of writing suitable for the purpose?

Structure and organisation

- Is there an opening paragraph that introduces the subject?
- Does the writing show features of text type?
- Has thought been given to layout and use of illustrations?

Grammar and style

- Are sentences correctly indicated by full stops, capital letters and question marks?
- Is the report coherent?
- Does the vocabulary reflect journalistic style?
- Is dialogue used?
- Are verb tenses accurate, moving between present and past?

Unit 26 Flood! 1

TASK: Plan and write story called 'Trapped'.
(This is linked to the subject matter covered in Shared Writing.)

Assessment Criteria

Purpose and audience

- Is the form of writing suitable for the purpose?

Structure and organisation

- Is there a clear beginning, middle and end?
- Is there a sense of dramatic effect?
- Does the story engage the readers' interest?

Grammar and style

- Is there good use of paragraphs?
- Are sentences correctly indicated by full stops, capital letters, question marks?
- Are a variety of connectives used?
- Is dialogue used?
- Does the writing contain precise detail?

Talking to Jamila Gavin

● STORY IDEAS

MAIN WRITING OBJECTIVE

- **To generate ideas by brainstorming, word association, etc.**   3.1 T9

Word and sentence level objective

- To investigate a range of devices for presenting texts.   3.1 S9

LESSON ONE

YOU WILL NEED

- **Pupil's Book** page 4
- **OHT 1** – Star Chart
- Flipchart
- **PCM 1** – ME star chart

MODEL TEXT

- Explain the lesson objective: *to find out how an author gets ideas for her stories.*

- Jamila Gavin was born in India. Many of her ideas for stories come from things that happened to her when she was little.

- Read the interview aloud, displaying the star chart and discussing it as you read the opening paragraph. Briefly discuss where pupils get their ideas for stories. Do they use their own lives?

- Why does Jamila Gavin ask so many questions when she is thinking of story ideas? *to find out lots of detail about the characters, to work out how they will behave*

- Why do pupils think her top tip is to 'write about things that really mean something to you'? *you'll know and understand it better*

- Discuss the stages of a story. Ask pupils to pick out the important words and phrases in paragraph 3. *beginning, problem, next, comes out right*

- Look at the questions on the star chart. Ask pupils to imagine the questions are about themselves. Encourage them to think of as many different answers as possible and note all the suggestions down. This process is called **brainstorming**. It helps you to collect as many ideas as you can before you write a story.

- Do pupils know the difference between FACT and FICTION? Their answers to the questions are FACTS because they are real. Authors often start with facts like these, but go on to write about imaginary people and events. This is FICTION.

Word and sentence level work

Ask pupils to explain what a star chart is in their own words. Why is this a useful way to make notes when brainstorming ideas?

Group activities: differentiation

All pupils make their own ME star chart using **PCM 1**.

Higher attainers could add some more questions of their own.

Plenary

Share star charts. What questions have pupils added? Discuss how one question leads to another and how this helps you to explore ideas.

ICT For activities linked to this lesson see **PAGE 102**

HOMEWORK

Pupils should take home their star charts and decide which of the ideas would make the best story. Encourage them to carry on asking questions and brainstorming ideas for the story on the back of the sheet.

Planning suggestion

This unit can form the basis of a week looking at ideas for stories. You could also link it to Unit 2, which includes a short extract from Jamila Gavin's story, *Kamla and Kate*.

LESSON TWO

SHARED WRITING

- Recap what a star chart is and how it can be used to get lots of ideas for your stories.

- Explain the lesson objective: *to use the star chart material to plan a story.*

- Display one homework example and read out some of the notes.

- Pick out a good idea, which could be a starting point for a story e.g. a scary event, a quarrel between best friends.

- Recap the main features of a story: setting, events, characters. Explain that you are all going to brainstorm ideas for these, and that every idea is important. Start to brainstorm and jot down all the ideas under the relevant headings on the OHT.

- Remind them that this is now fiction. Although they started with their own experience they should now start to make things up so that the story will be really interesting or exciting.

- Move on to plan the story. Keep it very simple. Ask pupils to think about how the story will start. What will happen in the story? How will the story end?

Group activities: differentiation

Pupils should use an idea from their star charts to brainstorm ideas for a story. They can use **PCM 2**. They should plan the events using a beginning, middle and end. **Lower attainers** could continue with the ideas from shared writing.

Guided writing. Help pupils make the transition from personal experience to fiction.

Plenary

Share some of the story ideas and plans. Do they sound interesting? Have pupils moved on from their original personal experience?

EXTENDED WRITING

Pupils use their notes and story plans to write a short story.

YOU WILL NEED
- Flipchart
- **OHT 2** – Story planner
- **PCM 2** – Story planner

ICT For activities linked to this lesson see **PAGE 102**

WATCH OUT FOR
▶ Inhibited brainstorming.
▶ Difficulty in making short notes.

2 Familiar Places ● STORY SETTING

MAIN WRITING OBJECTIVE

- **To develop the use of settings in stories by writing short descriptions of known places.** 3.1 T11

Word and sentence level objectives

- To understand and use a thesaurus to find synonyms. 3.1 W16
- To mark the end of a sentence with a full stop, and start a new one with a capital letter. 3.1 S12

LESSON ONE

MODEL TEXT

- Explain the lesson objective: *to look at examples of familiar settings in stories.*

- Explain that settings can give you clues to what a story is going to be about. For example, what would pupils expect to happen in an old house with a creaking door? Or a big barn full of hay? Or a castle?

- The writer tries to help us 'see' the setting clearly by using carefully chosen words and phrases to build up a picture.

- Read the extracts aloud. Ask pupils:

  – Where is the first extract set? *in the street, outside an empty house*

  – Can pupils 'see' the house? Ask them to describe it. What clues does the text give? *empty for ages, gardens . . . had become quite wild, over-grown*

  – Does Shakespeare Street seem the same or different? *possibly bigger; flats as well as houses, and a hypermarket; maybe no gardens/fields – astroturf*

- Are there any clues to what might happen in each of these stories?

- How do the writers make you want to read on? *the house is made to seem mysterious, asks a question at the end; we wonder if the football team will be any good*

Word and sentence level work

1 Ask pupils for two words to describe the garden. *wild, over-grown* Introduce the term synonym. Use a simple thesaurus to find synonyms for 'huge' and 'excited'.

2 How can you tell where one sentence ends and the next one begins? Ask pupils to read an example of a single sentence.

Group activities: differentiation

Pupils choose one extract and make notes about what might happen in the story. **Higher attainers** can think of other settings.

Plenary

Compare pupils' ideas for what might happen. How did they guess? Point out that the writer doesn't need to say a lot. We pick up on clues and imagine the rest.

YOU WILL NEED
- **Pupil's Book** page 6
- **PCM 3** – Homework

ICT For activities linked to this lesson see **PAGE 102**

HOMEWORK

Ask pupils to look carefully at their own street or the surroundings where they live, and write a few sentences to describe it. They can use **PCM 3** to help them.

40

Planning suggestion

This unit can be used as part of a week exploring settings. You could look at a range of familiar settings, and explore how writers use descriptive words and phrases to create a particular atmosphere.

LESSON TWO

SHARED WRITING

- Ask pupils to read the descriptions of their neighbourhood. Choose one and discuss what might happen if it was the setting for a story.

- Using the **Prompt Chart** recap what makes a good description of a setting.

- Explain the lesson objective: *to write a description of a familiar place.*

- Ask pupils to close their eyes and imagine the scene at break time. Encourage them to think about sounds and smells as well as what they see. Ask focused questions to encourage detail. What time of year do they imagine? Who is around? What noises are they making? Note all the ideas on the OHT.

- Explain that the same place can be made to feel very different. Discuss the effect of using different details. *cold and wet or bright and sunny; deserted playground or one full of children*

- Discuss some ideas for a story set in a playground. *a new pupil making a friend; a football match; a quarrel; an accident; a celebration.* Show pupils how to select details from the brainstorm to help set the scene. What kind of atmosphere will suit the story?

- Write the first sentence of a setting description together.

Group activities: differentiation

Pupils write their own description of a playground. They then read it to a partner and compare descriptions. **Higher attainers** should discuss what might happen in the story and write a sentence to make their partner want to read on. **Lower attainers** can use the frame on **PCM 4**.

Guided writing. Help **lower attainers** to select a few vivid details.

Plenary

Ask pupils to read their descriptions. Discuss the differences. Explain that even though it's the same place, every writer sees things differently. Much depends on what kind of story it's going to be.

EXTENDED WRITING

Pupils plan and write the rest of their story, concentrating on descriptions of setting.

YOU WILL NEED

- **OHT 3** – Settings Brainstorm
- **PCM 4** – Writing frame
- **Prompt Chart 1** – Story Writing (Setting)

ICT For activities linked to this lesson see **PAGE 102**

WATCH OUT FOR
- Bland adjectives.
- Lack of detail.

41

Cat Speak • REPORT

MAIN WRITING OBJECTIVE

- **To write a simple non-chronological report, from texts read, using notes to organise and present ideas.** 3.1 T23

Word and sentence level objective

- To use verb tenses with increasing accuracy in writing. 3.1 S4

LESSON ONE

MODEL TEXT

- Look at the extract together. Ask pupils what type of book it is from, how they know, and where they might find it. *non-fiction, contains information; about cats; in animal section of library*

- Explain the lesson objective: *to look at how a non-fiction book is organised*.

- Read the main heading, **Cat Speak**. Ask pupils to predict what the text is about.

- Read the first paragraph – the introduction. What does it tell us? *what the report is about*

- Look at the sub-headings. How do they tell us what the text is going to be about? *it's what the cat says, text then explains it* How does a cat say 'hello'?

- Discuss how the information is presented. *heading, sub-headings, bold print, numbered fact boxes, pictures*

- Why is the information presented this way? How does this help the reader?

- Ask a pupil to read the last section and explain that this is a summary.

- Is this report fact or fiction? Remind pupils that an information book is made up of facts.

Word and sentence level work

Ask pupils to pick out some of the verbs in the extract. What tense are they? Explain that when you are reporting information in this way, you should use the present tense. Change some present tense verbs into the past and discuss the effect.

Group activities: differentiation

All pupils answer question 1, using **PCM 5**. **Higher attainers** think of a sub-heading for box 2 in the Pupil's Book.

Guided reading. Help **lower attainers** to find information using numbered boxes and sub-headings.

Plenary

Ask pupils to suggest a sub-heading for box 2. Discuss why it is important to look for clues in pictures and headings.

YOU WILL NEED

- **Pupil's Book** pages 8–9
- **PCM 5** – What am I saying?
- **PCM 6** – Homework

 ICT For activities linked to this lesson see **PAGE 102**

HOMEWORK

Pupils use **PCM 6** to identify the features of non-fiction books. Confirm that they understand the terms.

Link to reading objectives

- To notice differences in the style and structure of fiction and non-fiction writing. 3.1 T18
- To locate information using contents, index, headings, sub-headings etc. 3.1 T19

Assumed prior knowledge

- Scan texts to find specific sections, using key words, phrases and sub-headings. 2.3 T16
- Skim read to say what a book is about. 2.3 T17
- To make simple notes from non-fiction texts. 2.3 T19

Planning suggestion

You could spend a week collecting, classifying and recording information related to the chosen topic.

LESSON TWO

SHARED WRITING

- Talk through the homework then recap how **'Cat Speak'** was organised using boxes, pictures and headings/sub-headings. Remind pupils that it is written in the present tense.

- Explain the lesson objective: *to write a short report.*

- Present a title linked to a class topic, or work in another subject. Fill in the title of the topic. Choose an area of the topic to write about. Make this the main heading.

- Brainstorm what pupils know about this area of the topic. Make notes on a flipchart. Explain to pupils that you are noting down the key facts only.

- With pupils, choose the most important aspects. Show them how to make these into sub-headings. Add these to the planner and make notes under each. 'Think aloud' as you do so. Tell pupils that they can use books to find more information if they wish.

- Model the writing of a short introduction. Stress the use of the present tense in report writing.

- Discuss what illustrations or diagrams would help to make the report clearer.

Group activities: differentiation

Working in pairs, pupils plan a non-chronological report about the topic from shared writing. They can use **PCM 7** to help them and a **Prompt Chart** is provided for extra support.
Lower attainers may continue to work on the plan from shared writing. All pupils should try to write a few sentences under each sub-heading.

Guided writing: Work with **lower attainers**. Model writing a section of the report. Show them how to make related sentences from brief notes.

Plenary

Invite some pupils to read out completed sections. Others should comment on the facts included and language.

EXTENDED WRITING

Pupils finish drafting their reports, adding a summary. Then they read it to others, checking for clarity, and revise.

YOU WILL NEED

- Books on a class topic
- Flipchart
- **OHT 4** – Report planner
- **PCM 7** – Report planner
- **Prompt Chart 2** – Report

ICT For activities linked to this lesson see **PAGE 102**

WATCH OUT FOR
- Slipping in to past tense.
- Irrelevant detail.

MAIN WRITING OBJECTIVE

- **To use reading as a model to write own passages of dialogue.**   3.1 T10

Word and sentence level objectives

- The basic conventions of speech punctuation.   3.1 S7
- To notice and investigate a range of devices for presenting text: speech bubbles.   3.1 S9
- Common vocabulary for introducing and concluding dialogue.   3.1 W19

LESSON ONE

YOU WILL NEED

- **Pupil's Book** pages 10–11
- **OHT 5** – Harry's Party
- **PCM 8** – Homework

MODEL TEXT

- Explain the lesson objective: *to look at dialogue in stories and how it is written and presented.*

- What do pupils know already about presenting dialogue? How does a writer show that someone's talking?

- Introduce the extract from *Harry's Party* by Chris Powling. Harry likes going to parties but he always causes trouble. In this extract he is getting ready for a fancy dress party. Read the extract aloud.

- Look at the dialogue in the first frame. How do we know who is speaking? *speech marks, 'said mum', new paragraph for Harry's answer*

- How else is dialogue presented? How do you know who's speaking? Discuss the use of speech bubbles in comics.

- Read Harry's dialogue again with expression. What can we tell about Harry's character from the way he speaks? *excited, eager, noisy*

Word and sentence level work

1 Teach the conventions of speech, marking speech marks, capital letters, 'said', new line for new speaker, questions, exclamations etc.

2 " 'Robocop?' said Mum." What word could replace said? *asked*

3 What would you need to add if you took the speech bubbles away? *speech marks, 'said mum', 'said Harry'* Ask a pupil to rewrite the dialogue in the speech bubbles using these conventions.

Group activities: differentiation

All pupils complete question 1 writing speech bubbles for Harry and his Mum. **Higher attainers** can go on to write more dialogue.

Guided reading. Help pupils to read the dialogue expressively, using the question and exclamation marks.

Plenary

Invite pupils to suggest speech bubble ideas. Scribe them on the board. Turn it into conventional dialogue by rubbing out the bubble and inserting speech marks and 'said'.

ICT For activities linked to this lesson see **PAGE 102**

HOMEWORK

Pupils complete the speech punctuation exercise on **PCM 8**.

Link to reading objective

- How dialogue is presented in stories e.g. through statements, questions, exclamations; how paragraphing is used to organise dialogue.   3.1 T2

Assumed prior knowledge

- To identify and understand speech marks.   2.2 S6
- Exclamation marks.   2.1 S3
- Question marks.   1.3 S7
- Using dialogue in sustained stories.   2.3 T10

Planning suggestion

You could use this unit as part of a week looking at the presentation of dialogue. You could use an example of a pupil's writing for a shared session on revising and editing with particular emphasis on dialogue.

LESSON TWO

SHARED WRITING

- Spend a few minutes looking back at the homework. Review the rules for writing dialogue.

- Explain the lesson objective: *to write dialogue for a new story called Harry Moves House.*

- Introduce the new extract, which is from another book in the same series called *Harry Moves House*. Harry's mum is expecting a baby and they are going to move house. Harry isn't looking forward to it and his dad tries to cheer him up.

- Read the extract together. Point out the speech bubbles and ask pupils to say what you will need to add to the dialogue if you take the bubbles away.

- Start to demonstrate this on the OHT by adding speech marks etc to the first speech bubble. Does the question mark go inside or outside the speech marks? *inside* Why? *because Harry's asking a question – it's part of the words he says*

- Write the text out in full as conventional dialogue: 'Can I?' asked Harry.

- With pupils, write the next two speech bubbles as conventional dialogue. Remind them about using a new line for a new speaker.

Group activities: differentiation

Pupils read the next part on the extract on **PCM 9** and change the speech bubbles into conventional dialogue, using speech marks, new paragraphs and indicating the speaker. **Lower attainers** can use **PCM 10** and simply add the necessary details.

Guided writing. Introduce alternatives for 'said'.

Plenary

Share work in progress. Encourage pupils to read out their dialogue expressively. Recap the rules for written dialogue and speech bubbles.

EXTENDED WRITING

Pupils imagine what will happen when Harry meets his new baby sister, and write some lines of dialogue between Harry and his parents.

YOU WILL NEED

- Flipchart
- **OHT 6** – Speech bubbles
- **PCM 9** – Speech bubbles
- **PCM 10** – Dialogue

 For activities linked to this lesson see **PAGE 102**

 WATCH OUT FOR
- ► Forgetting rule for new paragraphs.
- ► Speech marks incorrectly placed.

5 Ace Dragon Ltd • PLAYSCRIPT

MAIN WRITING OBJECTIVE

- **To write simple playscripts.**   3.1 T15

Word and sentence level objectives

- To secure knowledge of question and exclamation marks.   3.1 S6
- The basic conventions of speech punctuation.   3.1 S7

LESSON ONE

MODEL TEXT

- Are pupils familiar with playscripts? How are they different from stories?

- Explain the lesson objective: *to prepare a reading of a playscript.*

- Look at the playscript together. Focus on the layout, marking the OHT as you discuss it. Explain that playscripts are written entirely in dialogue. The words in bold tell you who is speaking. There are no speech marks, and there is no need to say 'said ...'.

- The words in italics are stage directions. They tell the actors what to do or how to say their lines, and what is happening on stage.

- Read through the playscript. Choose a pupil to take John's part. Stress the dragon's grumpiness and conceit as you read. Ask pupils:
  – Who are the characters in the play? *John and Ace (a dragon)*
  – Which words tell us how some lines should be spoken? *grumpily, excitedly*
  – What sort of boy do you think John is? *curious, adventurous*
  – How do you think Ace should say the line, 'I can make fire come out of my nose and mouth.'? *proudly, eagerly*

- Why are the stage directions important? *they explain what is happening, and tell the performers what to do*

Word and sentence level work

1 Ask pupils to find two questions asked by the dragon. Practise reading questions with expression.

2 Look for the exclamation mark in the play. How should this line be said aloud?

Group activities: Differentiation

Pupils work in pairs to prepare a reading of the play, marking the script on **PCM 11**.

Guided reading. Provide support to **lower attainers** to help them decide how the lines should be read.

Plenary

Invite a couple of pairs to perform the play. Evaluate the performance.

YOU WILL NEED

- **Pupils Book** page 12
- **OHT 7** – Ace Dragon Ltd
- **PCM 11** – Playscript
- **PCM 12** – Homework

  ICT For activities linked to this lesson see **PAGE 102**

HOMEWORK

Pupils read the next part of Ace Dragon Ltd on **PCM 12** and add in the missing punctuation.

Link to reading objectives	
● To read, prepare and present playscripts.	3.1 T4
● To recognise the key differences between prose and playscripts by looking at dialogue, stage directions, layout.	3.1 T5

Assumed prior knowledge	
● Role play and dialogue.	2.2 T7
● Recognising different ways of presenting texts.	2.2 S7
● Knowledge of story elements, including dialogue.	2.3 T 10

Planning suggestion

This unit can be linked to Unit 4 and used as part of a week looking at different ways of presenting dialogue. Alternatively it could be used as part of a week introducing and exploring simple playscripts.

LESSON TWO

SHARED WRITING

- Spend a few minutes reviewing the homework. Why is punctuation so important for people reading parts in a play? *shows how lines should be read*

- What happened in scene 2? How did it end? *Ace running out of petrol*

- Explain the lesson objective: *to look at the next part of the story and write it as a playscript.*

- Read through the next part of the story together.

- Using the writing frame, fill in the title and scene number (3). Ask pupils to suggest some details that will set the scene.

- Ask pupils who speaks first. Write in his name, emphasising the use of the colon. What does he say? Write it out, reminding pupils that you don't need to use 'said'.

- Write out the next few lines of dialogue. Ask pupils to think about how they would say the lines. Remind them to use ? and ! as clues.

- End with a stage direction for the line 'They landed on the moon just as Ace ran out of petrol'.

Group activities: Differentiation

Pupils work in mixed ability groups, writing out the rest of the extract as a play. They can use **PCM 13** for support. If they wish they can go on to think about what might happen next and write some more dialogue for Ace and John.

Guided writing. Work on the layout of the script, and accuracy of punctuation.

Plenary

Invite a group to show the layout of their work, then to perform it for the class. Evaluate the layout against the **Prompt Chart**.

EXTENDED WRITING

Pupils plan another adventure for John and Ace Dragon, and write it out as a short playscript.

YOU WILL NEED
- **Pupil's Book** page 13
- **OHT 8** – Playscript writing frame
- **PCM 13** – Playscript writing frame
- **Prompt Chart 3** – Playscripts

ICT For activities linked to this lesson see **PAGE 102**

WATCH OUT FOR
▶ The inclusion of 'said' and speech marks in the playscript.

MAIN WRITING OBJECTIVE

- **To write a simple non-chronological report from own experience, using notes made to organise.** 3.1 T23

Word and sentence level objectives

- To use verb tenses with increasing accuracy in writing. 3.1 S4

LESSON ONE

YOU WILL NEED

- **Pupil's Book** page 14
- **PCM 14** – Word web
- **PCM 15** – Flamborough
- **PCM 16** – Homework

MODEL TEXT

- Explain the lesson objective: *to look at two reports based on personal experience.*

The reports are about the writers' favourite people or places.

- Read Neil's piece aloud. Ask pupils:
  - What does the first paragraph of the report tell you? *what the report is about, it's an introduction*
  - What does Neil's grandad look like? *small and fat*
  - Why do you think Neil likes him so much? Ask pupils to pick out the key words and phrases from the text. *kind, jolly, sings with me, takes me walking, funny – makes people laugh*

- Now read Karen's report about her favourite place. Ask pupils:
  - Where is Flamborough? *East coast*
  - What would you see if you went there? Again encourage pupils to pick out key words. *lighthouse, rock pools, caves, cliffs, birds*

- Discuss how Karen has organised her information into paragraphs. She uses them to group key facts.

Word and sentence level work

1 Look at Neil's report and make a list of all the things his grandad does. *listens, sings, walking, tells, reading, snores*
Remind pupils that these are verbs. What tense are they?

2 If Neil was writing about how things used to be, how would these words change? *past tense verbs: listened, sang, walked etc*

Group activities: differentiation

Lower attainers write a word web about Neil's grandad using **PCM 14**.
Higher attainers make notes about Flamborough on **PCM 15**. If they have time they can also complete the word web.

Guided reading. Help pupils to pick out key words and phrases.

Plenary

Pupils report back their findings about Neil's grandad. Ask a group to read out their list of things to do in Flamborough. Discuss who might read Karen's report. *people who are thinking of visiting*

 ICT For activities linked to this lesson see **PAGE 103**

HOMEWORK

Pupils read the extract on **PCM 16**, then change the verbs from past to present tense.

Link to reading objective

- To read information passages, and identify key points by noting key words and phrases. 3.1 T21

Assumed prior knowledge

- To make simple notes e.g. key words. 2.3 T19
- To scan a text for key words and phrases. 2.3 T16
- To use commas in lists. 2.3 S4
- To use standard forms of verbs. 2.3 S3

Planning suggestion

This unit can be used as part of a week working on non-chronological reports. It links to Unit 3.

LESSON TWO

YOU WILL NEED
- Flipchart
- **OHT 9** – Report frame
- **Prompt Chart 2** – Report

SHARED WRITING

- Go through the homework. Explain that reports are usually written in the present tense because they describe things as they are now.

- Explain the lesson objective: *to write a report about a familiar person or place.*

- With pupils choose a person you all know well, or a place you have visited together. Brainstorm everything you know about the person or place. Make notes on a flipchart.

- Discuss categories into which you can group the information, e.g. *Place – where it is, what you see, what you do, special features; Person – appearance, things they do, what they are like.*

- Write these as paragraph headings. Explain that these will guide the writing of the report.

- With pupils underline the key points (words and phrases) that you will include in paragraph 2 and note them on the planner. Repeat the excercise for paragraphs 3 and 4.

- Discuss what should go in the introductory paragraph and model writing it. Emphasise the use of the present tense.

- Discuss how you could end the report – summarise why you like the person or place.

Group activities: Differentiation

Pupils continue writing the report begun in shared writing. **Lower attainers** can copy the introductory sentences, **higher attainers** should write their own. You can display the **Prompt Chart** for support.

Guided writing. Work with **lower attainers** scribing a group report. Show them how to use the brainstorm notes, grouping and underlining information. Stress the use of present tense

Plenary

Invite pupils to share their work in progress. Ask the others to comment on the most interesting parts. Is it in the present tense?

EXTENDED WRITING

Pupils finish writing their reports, then read them aloud to a partner and discuss which bits could be improved. They then revise it.

ICT For activities linked to this lesson see **PAGE 103**

WATCH OUT FOR !
- Inconsistent use of present tense.
- Poor grouping of information.

7

Rhythm Machine • SHAPE POEMS

MAIN WRITING OBJECTIVE

- **To invent calligrams and a range of shape poems selecting appropriate words and presentation.**　　3.1 T14

Word and sentence level objective

- To investigate a range of devices for presenting text.　　3.1 S9

LESSON ONE

MODEL TEXT

- Explain the lesson objective: *to look at a range of different 'word shape' poems.*

- In word shape poems the words are used to make a shape.

- Look at the selection of poems together. How do 'Tunnel' and 'Tyrannosaurus Rex' work? *they are made of only one word and the word is in the shape of its meaning* Ask a pupil to trace the letters making up 'Tunnel' with a finger.

- Look at 'Tyrannosaurus Rex'. What are the legs made out of? *capital R for back legs and the x for its small front legs* How is the E like its head? *the prongs of the capital E are like its jaws*

- How is 'Snake' different from these other two poems? *it uses lots of words to make the shape and describes the snake*

- Now read 'Rhythm Machine' together. Ask pupils to comment on things they notice about some of the words, e.g. *'loud' is in large writing and the lines around it look like echoes; 'trumpet' and 'drum' are in the shape of the instruments; the letters in 'volume' get bigger etc.*

- Point out how the words 'soft', 'humming', 'loud' and 'strumming' are written as if to give you the **feeling** of the word.

- Explain that this kind of shape poem is called a calligram. The shape of the letters reflects the **meaning** of the word.

Word and sentence level work

Ask pupils to suggest ways of writing 'angry', 'bouncy' and 'hard' in ways that suggest the meaning (calligrams).

Group activities: differentiation

Working in pairs, pupils choose a favourite word shape poem and discuss why they like it best. They then try to think of other ways to write the words. **Higher attainers** can go on to write some word shapes of their own.

Plenary

Invite pairs of pupils to justify their favourite word shape poems, then take a class vote.

YOU WILL NEED

- **Pupil's Book** pages 16–17
- **PCM 17** – Homework

 For activities linked to this lesson see **PAGE 103**

HOMEWORK

Using **PCM 17** pupils think of their own word shapes for different musical instruments.

Link to reading objective

- To distinguish between rhyming and non-rhyming poetry; to comment on the impact of layout.   3.1 T7

Assumed prior knowledge

- Experience of a range of poetry.
- Words and phrases that create humour and sound effects.   2.3 T8

Planning suggestion

This initial work on shape poems can be continued through the week. You can look at a range of different types of shape poems, and pupils' work can be used for shared reading and writing – working on revising texts.

LESSON TWO

SHARED WRITING

- Look at some of the musical instrument word shapes.
- Explain the lesson objective: *to look at more calligrams and write some together.*
- Remind pupils that calligrams are poems where the shape of the letters reflects the meaning of the word.
- Read 'Holiday Memories'. Ask pupils to comment on how the way some of the words are written reflects the meaning of the word.
- How might they improve on 'fed up' or 'fantastic'?
- What effect do the shadows have on 'Roasting'?
- Explain that you are now going to start writing some calligrams together. Decide on a subject which will arouse plenty of strong feelings, e.g. going to the dentist, or a Haunted House.
- Brainstorm the words you might include and ask pupils to think about how you would illustrate them, for example: creaking, ghost, frightened, spooky etc.
- Write these words out on a flipchart. Encourage pupils to think about the layout. You could use colour for extra effect.

Group activities: differentiation

All pupils work on their own calligram poems, using the ideas from shared writing if they wish. Remind them to try to convey the meaning of the word. **Lower attainers** can use the writing frame on **PCM 18** for support.

Guided writing. Encourage a variety of strategies (shape, colour, size etc) to make the look of the words reflect the meaning.

Plenary

Display some work in progress and ask for comments and ideas for improvement. Does the way the words are written reflect the meaning?

EXTENDED WRITING

Pupils use their best ideas to write calligram or shape poems. They then make final copies for a class collection.

YOU WILL NEED

- **OHT 10** – Holiday Memories
- Flipchart
- **PCM 18** – Calligram writing frame

ICT For activities linked to this lesson see **PAGE 103**

WATCH OUT FOR
▶ Difficulty in representing abstract words.

51

8

Frogs and Toads • INFORMATION

MAIN WRITING OBJECTIVE

- **To make a simple record of information from texts read, e.g. by completing a chart of information discovered, listing key words.**

  3.1 T22

Word and sentence level objective

- To notice and investigate a range of devices for presenting texts.

  3.1 S9

LESSON ONE

MODEL TEXT

- Explain the lesson objective: *to look at different ways of recording and presenting information.*

- Ask pupils to glance quickly at the pages in their books. What is the information about? *frogs and toads*

- How is it presented? *chart, labelled picture, Fact Tree*

Look at 'Spot the difference!' Ask half the class to read the 'Frog' column, and half to read 'Toad'.
  – What information is recorded in the chart? *appearance/movement*
  – Why is the chart a useful way of showing information? *makes it easy to compare things*
  – How is the text presented? *in note form, using key words and facts*

- Look at the labelled picture of the toad. Do you think this a good way of presenting information? Why?

- Look at the Fact-Tree. A group of children researched information and recorded it this way. Ask pupils:
  – What main areas of information did the group research? *where toads live, what they look like, life cycle, movements, food*
  – Where would you expect to see a toad? *garden, field, wood, pond*

Word and sentence level work

1 Look at the different ways of presenting information. How easy are the reports to understand? Which report is the easiest to get information from and why?

2 Look at 'Spot the difference'. What other information would be useful? *labelled picture of frog, picture showing movement*

Group activities: differentiation

Lower attainers complete question 1 using **PCM 19**.

Higher attainers use **PCM 20** to re-organise the information on the Toad Fact Tree into a fact-web. They then complete the short report about toads.

Plenary

Ask two **lower attainers** to show and talk about their labelled frogs. Invite a **higher attainer** to read their completed report.

YOU WILL NEED

- **Pupil's Book** pages 18–19
- **PCM 19** – Frog
- **PCM 20** – Toad

ICT For activities linked to this lesson see **PAGE 103**

HOMEWORK

Ask pupils to look for information on labels, in magazines etc. which show information in different ways. Ask them to choose one or two that they think are really clear and bring them in.

Link to reading objective

- To look at the way information is presented by comparing a variety of information texts.

3.1 T20

Assumed prior knowledge

- To use a contents page to find way about text. 2.3 T15
- To scan a text to find specific sections, key words, phrases and sub-headings. 2.3 T16
- To skim read title, contents, illustrations and headings, to say what a book is about. 2.3 T17
- To make simple notes from non-fiction texts, e.g. key words. 2.3 T19

Planning suggestion

Pupils can continue this work through the week, recording information from their reading. They can use their work for a session in which the class evaluates different ways of recording information.

LESSON TWO

SHARED WRITING

- Display the information pupils have brought from home. Note the different formats: charts, labels, lists, headings, diagrams etc.

- Explain the lesson objective: *to record information about a recent class topic.*

- Remind them of some of the information they learnt about the topic. Think of two subjects within that topic that you could compare, e.g. two different insects; past and present.

- Write the two subjects as headings on the OHT. Ask pupils to suggest some key characteristics that they could compare, e.g. food, where or how they live, appearance. Add these in as sub-headings.

- With pupils, brainstorm facts about one of the subjects, using the sub-headings to help you. Add them to the chart. Explain that you are picking out key words and writing the information in note form NOT in sentences.

- Explain to pupils that they will be writing key points about the second subject during group activities.

Group activities: differentiation

Pupils work in mixed ability groups, brainstorming and noting down key facts about the second subject using **PCM 21**. They could use books and other information to help them if needed. They then copy down the facts from shared writing and start to think about how they would present the information. Differentiation will be by outcome.

Guided writing. Help pupils to think of different ways of presenting the information on their chart.

Plenary

Invite pupils to share their ideas for presenting the information. Discuss which ways would be most suitable and why.

EXTENDED WRITING

Pupils decide on the best way to present their information, then make an information sheet based on their notes. Encourage them to use labelled pictures or diagrams on their final version.

YOU WILL NEED

- **OHT 11** – Comparison chart
- **PCM 21** – Comparison chart
- Books and other information on a recent class topic

ICT For activities linked to this lesson see **PAGE 103**

WATCH OUT FOR

- Copying out whole sentences from source.
- Lack of understanding of what 'key facts' are.

53

Like and Hate • REPEATING PHRASES

MAIN WRITING OBJECTIVE

- **To write poems using simple patterns with words and repetitive phrases.**   3.1 T13

Word and sentence level objectives

- To use a thesaurus to find synonyms.   3.1 W16
- Collecting and classifying verbs.   3.1 S3

LESSON ONE

MODEL TEXT

- Explain the lesson objective: *to look at 'like' and 'hate' poems that use repeating phrases.*

- Talk briefly about foods that pupils really like or hate. Encourage them to suggest vivid adjectives and verbs to describe their feelings.

- Read aloud the extracts from the two poems by Michael Rosen, relishing every word and emphasising the crisp sounds. Stress the speech rhythms. Ask pupils:
  – What does the poet hate most about tomatoes? What does he like?
  – Which descriptions do you agree with?
  – The poems don't rhyme and sound like speech. How do you know that they are poems? *short lines, rhythm, repeated phrases*

- Now read through 'Battle Lines'. Can pupils pick out the repeated phrases? *What I hate about spiders/What I like about spiders*

- Ask pupils to pick out the 'hate' words about spiders. *big black hairy legs, hide in corners, creep up on you* What words are used to show 'like'? *beautiful silky webs, the way they make people scream*

Word and sentence level work

Ask pupils to pick out some of the verbs in 'Tomato 1'. *sticks, slide, eat* Can they think of any other verbs beginning with 's' to describe eating a tomato? Show pupils how to use a thesaurus to look up synonyms. *slurp, slop, slither, scoff*

Group activities: differentiation

Pupils work in pairs to practise reading one of the poems aloud with expression. Encourage them to think about the emotions of like and hate and to convey them in their reading.

Higher attainers can go on to look up and list synonyms for eating.

Plenary

Ask some pupils to read the poems aloud. Other pupils should evaluate the speech patterns and rhythms.

YOU WILL NEED
- **Pupil's Book** pages 21–22

ICT For activities linked to this lesson see **PAGE 103**

HOMEWORK

Ask pupils to think of one thing that they really like, and one thing that they really hate. It could be animals or foods or games or something else. They should also make notes of their reasons.

Link to reading objective

● To read aloud and recite poems; to discuss the impact of verbs
and adjectives.   3.1 T6

Assumed prior knowledge

● Poems with pattern and rhythm.   2.2 T9

Planning suggestion

This unit could be used as
part of a week looking at
poetry, focusing on
powerful descriptions. You
may wish to look at a
selection of poems from *I
Like that Stuff* by Roger
McGough before asking
children to write more
poetry of their own.

LESSON TWO

SHARED WRITING

● Explain the lesson objective: *to write a Hate/Like poem using 'Battle Lines' as a model.*

● Read 'Battle Lines' again. Notice the pattern of the verses. How are they arranged? *hate and like alternately, same pattern but different number of lines*

● Ask pupils to feedback some of their homework ideas. Choose one which will provoke strong feelings of liking and hating as the subject for the shared poem.

● Brainstorm all the things you might like or hate about it.

● Choose one thing that pupils really hate about the subject and model writing the first verse. Ask pupils to suggest some powerful verbs to convey the strong feelings.

● Read the verse aloud as you write. Does it sound convincing? Cross out or change some of the words. Spend time hunting for the exact words you want to use. Ask pupils to use a thesaurus to help you.

● Do the same for the next verse, choosing something pupils really like. Again encourage pupils to find the right words to describe feelings, and keep reading through the poem aloud as you write.

Group activities: differentiation

Pupils use their homework notes to write a hate/like poem using **PCM 22**. **Lower attainers** can write one or two verses only, or you could work with them and scribe a group poem.

Guided writing. Encourage the use of a thesaurus to find synonyms.

Plenary

Share work in progress, evaluating the pattern, rhythm, and the accuracy of the descriptions. Can pupils suggest other words that might work better?

EXTENDED WRITING

Pupils finish their poems and then swap with a partner. They evaluate the strength of feelings and how well they are expressed. They then revise the poems and produce a final version for a class display.

YOU WILL NEED
● **Pupil's Book** page 22
● **OHT 12** – Writing frame
● **PCM 22** – Writing frame

 For activities linked
to this lesson see
PAGE 103

WATCH OUT FOR
▶ Bland verbs and
description.
▶ Difficulty in capturing
speech rhythms.

10 Once Upon a Time ... the End

● STORY OPENINGS AND ENDINGS

MAIN WRITING OBJECTIVES

- **To collect sentences/phrases for story openings and endings.** 3.1 T12
- **To begin to organise stories into paragraphs.** 3.1 T16

Word and sentence level objectives

- To write in complete sentences. 3.1 S11
- To punctuate sentences with a capital letter and full stop. 3.1 S12

LESSON ONE

MODEL TEXT

- Explain the lesson objective: *to evaluate a selection of story openings and endings.*

- Pupils will know 'Once upon a time' and 'Happy ever after', but they don't always make the most exciting opening or ending of a story. Ask pupils how else you could begin a story?

- Discuss the key features of a good story opening. You need to set the scene and introduce characters, but the most important thing is to get the reader hooked.

- Read aloud the three story openings. Discuss each one in turn.
  - How does the extract introduce character?
  - How does the extract introduce setting?
  - How does the extract make us want to go on reading?
  - What kind of story do you think each one is going to be? What clues tell you?
  - What is different about the second extract? *it uses dialogue*

- Discuss which story pupils would most like to read and why.

- Explain that sometimes story endings are a bit of a let-down. e.g. ... *and then we all went home.* OR *... then it was time for bed.*

- How do pupils end their own stories? Do they find it difficult? Why?

- Discuss the features of a good story opening and ending on the **Prompt Chart**.

Word and sentence level work

1 Use opening 1 to reinforce the rules for sentence punctuation.

2 Use opening 2 to recap the rules for writing speech. Remind them about paragraphs for dialogue.

Group activities: differentiation

Working in pairs, pupils match the story openings to the right endings on **PCM 23**. **Higher attainers** also choose one story and make notes about what happened in between.

Plenary

Ask which endings fit which opening. Take a vote on the favourite story and discuss reasons.

YOU WILL NEED

- **Pupil's Book** pages 24–25
- **OHT 13** – Story openings
- **PCM 23** – Story endings
- **PCM 24** – Homework
- **Prompt Chart 4** – Openings and Endings

ICT For activities linked to this lesson see **PAGE 104**

HOMEWORK

Pupils use the extract on **PCM 24** to practise punctuating sentences.

Link to reading objective

● To express views about a story, identifying specific words and phrases to support views

Assumed prior knowledge

● Story event
● Story settin
● Comparing

Planning suggestion

This section be used as work on It can be 1 and 2, or d 12.

LESSON TWO

SHARED WRITING

● Using the **Prompt Chart**, recap the features of good story openings and endings.

● Explain the lesson objective: *to write your own story opening and ending, using the first story as a model.*

● Brainstorm a new name for the main character, maybe a boy.

● Josie was the 'strongest little girl in the world'. What is special about this boy? Why can he do tricks? *cleverest, tallest, greediest, fastest*

● Think of some tricks the character could do. *run all the way to town in three seconds; eat twenty-three helpings of school pudding etc*

● What is the best trick going to be? It needs to be something that will make a good story. You won't actually write about it, just build up to it.

● When and where will the best trick happen? Put clues into the second paragraph: It happened when … *someone's football got stuck on the roof of the school; a house in the town set on fire*

● Discuss what might happen in the story. How will the story end? Using the original as a model, jot down some ideas.

Group activities: differentiation

Pupils work in pairs to write story openings and endings. **Lower attainers** can use the writing frame on **PCM 25** but should come up with some original ideas. **Higher attainers** could use one of the other models – dialogue, description, ending on a question.

Guided writing. Work with **higher attainers** on the use of paragraphs for different speakers, and for changes of subject, place or time.

Plenary

Read some story openings and evaluate them against the **Prompt Chart**. Ask pupils to guess what might happen in the stories before listening to the endings. Did they fit the openings? Were they good endings?

EXTENDED WRITING

Pupils could practise writing more story openings and endings using different models.

YOU WILL NEED

● OHT 14 – Writing frame
● **PCM 25** – Writing frame
● **Prompt Chart 4** –
  Openings and endings

OHT
14

PCM
25

ICT For activities linked to this lesson see **PAGE 104**

WATCH OUT FOR
▶ Difficulty in thinking of good endings.
▶ Lack of paragraphing.
▶ Poor punctuation.

11

Who? What? Where?

● STORY PLANNING

MAIN WRITING OBJECTIVE

- **To plan main points as a structure for a story; to discuss different methods of planning.**　　　3.2 T6

Word and sentence level objective

- Identifying and experimenting with adjectives.　　　3.2 S2

LESSON ONE

MODEL TEXT

- Explain the lesson objective: *to look at different ways of planning stories.*

- Writers plan their stories in lots of different ways. A story plan is like a skeleton – just the bare bones – but it gives the story a shape. You flesh it out when you start writing and adding the detail.

- Recap some of the ideas from Unit 1 – brainstorming, questioning, making notes, charts and diagrams to get all your ideas down.

- Look at the different ways in which Vicky and Jason planned their stories. Jason started by planning the characters for his story, brainstorming lots of adjectives to describe them. How do pupils think that will help when he writes the story? *he'll have a clear idea of how the characters might behave* What doesn't his plan cover? *what will happen in the story or how it will end*

- Vicky's plan shows what's going to happen – the **plot** as well as the characters. Can pupils work it out? *characters go to the moon, meet an alien, have a fight* Does she plan enough about the characters? *not really – they all look the same, so it might be a bit boring* Does she plan how she will end the story? *yes, but it's not very clear*

- Why do you think it is important to plan the ending? *to give the story direction*

Word and sentence level work

Introduce/recap the term *adjective* – words used to describe things. Look at Vicky's plan and ask pupils to suggest adjectives to describe her characters.

Group activities: differentiation

Pupils work in pairs to evaluate the two planning formats, using **PCM 26**. **Higher attainers** can go on to question 2. Make it clear that pupils are not being asked whether they like the story ideas, but whether they like that way of planning.

Plenary

Ask pupils to suggest the good and bad points about each planning method. Discuss the different things you need to think about when you plan a story. Use the **Prompt Chart**.

YOU WILL NEED

- **Pupil's Book** pages 27–28
- **PCM 26–** Planning stories
- **PCM 27–** Homework
- **Prompt Chart 1** – Story Writing

ICT For activities linked to this lesson see **PAGE 104**

HOMEWORK

Pupils complete the story planning questionnaire on **PCM 27.**

Link to reading objectives	
• To identify typical story themes.	3.2 T2
• To identify and discuss main characters.	3.2 T3

Assumed prior knowledge	
• Basic story elements.	1.2 T10
• To write story settings.	2.2 T13
• To write character profiles.	2.2 T14
• Unit 1 – Talking to Jamila Gavin.	

Planning suggestion

This unit can be used as part of extended work on planning and writing stories, and links to other units on character, setting, story maps and sequels.

LESSON TWO

SHARED WRITING

• Explain the lesson objective: *to plan your own story.*

• Share pupils responses to the homework questionnaire. What do they find easiest to do? What do they find difficult?

• Explain to pupils that a useful tool for planning a story is a story starter. Display the OHT and ask pupils to suggest the title of a familiar story, but changing the characters names e.g. Mother Hen, Little Blue Riding Hood, Zak and the Beanstalk.

• Choose one that pupils know well and start to brainstorm ideas for the setting, character and plot. Show them how to write brief notes and key words under each of the questions on the planner.

• Begin to structure the plot. Ask pupils for ideas for the beginning, middle and end of the story and make notes on the planner.

• Discuss the things that pupils find most difficult about planning and spend a bit more time on this before sending them off to plan their own stories.

Group activities: differentiation

Pupils use **PCM 28** to plan their own stories. **Lower attainers** could base their story on a familiar tale or continue the work from shared writing.

Guided writing. Help pupils with the aspects of planning that they find most difficult.

Plenary

Ask some children to share their story plans. Talk about how helpful they found the story starter. Which planning format do they like best? Take a vote.

EXTENDED WRITING

Pupils use one of the other model planning methods to plan a story, and decide which way works best.
Alternatively, you could ask them to write a story based on their plan. They can then evaluate the effectiveness of the plan.

YOU WILL NEED

• **OHT 15** – Story Starter
• **PCM 28** – Story Starter
• **Prompt Chart 1** – Story Writing

⚠ WATCH OUT FOR

▶ Writing the whole story instead of making brief notes.

12

A Poor Widow's Son ● CHARACTER

MAIN WRITING OBJECTIVE

- **To write character portraits using story text to describe behaviour and characteristics and presenting in a variety of ways.** 3.2 T8

Word and sentence level objectives

- To explore opposites. 3.2 W24
- Adjectives. 3.2 S2

LESSON ONE

MODEL TEXT

- Explain the lesson objective: *to read and discuss some character descriptions.*

- Traditional stories often have typical characters. Ask pupils to suggest some, e.g. *prince, princess, woodcutter, giant, witch*

- Brainstorm some adjectives often used to describe them. *beautiful, brave, handsome, kind, fierce, cruel, greedy, dangerous*

- Read the character descriptions aloud. Ask pupils:
  - Which characters would you expect to be the goodies? *princess, prince, poor widow's son*
  - Why? *beautiful princesses are usually good; the prince is handsome and brave; the poor widow's son is cheerful though poor*
  - Which characters do you think are baddies, and why? *stepmothers tend to be evil in stories; giant could be a baddie – sounds dangerous; tall stranger sounds suspicious*

- Point out that the adjectives can give us clues as to what the characters are like. Ask pupils to pick some out.

- Explain that what the characters say and do can also give you clues to the plot. Ask pupils to find examples. *the widow's son sets off to try his luck; the giant says he'll kill the prince; the stranger asks if he can help but sounds suspicious*

Word and sentence level work

Ask pupils to define 'adjective'. Brainstorm more adjectives to describe the characters. Think of some opposites, e.g. *cheerful/gloomy, poor/rich* Change the adjectives in the extracts to their opposites. How does this change our view of the characters and what might happen in the story?

Group activities: differentiation

Pupils work in pairs using **PCM 29** to build up character webs. **Higher attainers** could also make webs for other typical story characters.

Plenary

Make a list of adjectives from pupils' suggestions. Leave the list displayed for the following literacy lesson.

YOU WILL NEED

- **Pupil's Book** pages 30–31
- **OHT 16** – Character extracts
- **PCM 29** – Character web
- **PCM 30** – Homework

 ICT For activities linked to this lesson see **PAGE 104**

HOMEWORK

Ask pupils to make a list of characters they know from traditional tales and to divide them into goodies and baddies.

Pupils needing further work on adjectives could find opposites for those listed on **PCM 30**.

Planning suggestion

This unit can be used as part of an extended period of work on story planning and traditional tales. It links to other units on planning and story writing, and to Unit 16 Too Much Searching.

LESSON TWO

SHARED WRITING

- Recap yesterday's discussion about characters and how adjectives can help us find out what they are like.

- Explain the lesson objective: *to build up a character portrait.*

- Ask pupils what a portrait is. *a picture of a person* It can be created using words.

- Ask pupils to suggest some characters from traditional tales. Make a list under the headings 'Goodies' and 'Baddies', e.g. Cinderella, Wicked Witch, Aladdin, the Big Bad Wolf

- Explain that you are going to design a 'Wanted' poster for one of the baddies. Choose one together and ask pupils to describe him/her. Draw on the list of adjectives from the previous lesson.

- Fill in some of the details on the 'Wanted' poster. Remind pupils that the description will need to be really accurate, so that the baddy can be found! Concentrate on the key details.

Group activities: differentiation

Lower attainers design a 'Wanted' poster (**PCM 31**) for a baddy.
Higher attainers design a 'Missing Person' poster (**PCM 32**) for a goody. All pupils can swap their work with a partner and discuss possible improvements.

Guided writing. Help pupils to find descriptive adjectives.

Plenary

Invite pupils to show their posters and to explain why that character is a goody or a baddy. Add any particularly good adjectives to the class list.

EXTENDED WRITING

Pupils make a finished copy of their poster for a 'Goodies and Baddies' gallery.

YOU WILL NEED

- Flipchart headed 'Goodies' and 'Baddies'
- **OHT 17** – Wanted poster
- **PCM 31** – Wanted poster
- **PCM 32** – Missing person poster

ICT For activities linked to this lesson see **PAGE 104**

WATCH OUT FOR
► Lack of imagination in adjectives work.

Memo to me ● NOTEMAKING

MAIN WRITING OBJECTIVE

- To discuss and identify the purpose for which particular notes will be used; identifying audience; using simple formats to capture key points.　　　　　　　　　　　　　　　　　3.2 T17

Word and sentence level objective

- To experiment with deleting words in sentences to see which are essential to meaning.　　　　　　　　　　　　　　　　　3.2 S9

LESSON ONE

MODEL TEXT

- Explain the lesson objective: *to look at the importance of key words when writing notes, and to discuss the purpose of notemaking.*

- Ask pupils what kind of notes they or their families make for themselves, e.g. *reminders, shopping lists, 'to do' lists etc*

- Where do they write them? *hand, scrap of paper, memo board, notebook*

- Notemaking is generally for **remembering** things. Introduce the term 'memo'. Often you have to make notes quickly, so they need to be short, but you have to be able to understand them later.

- Cover up the poem on the OHT, and look at the notes. Explain that Justin looked closely at the class snails, then he made these notes for himself. Ask pupils:
  - What key points did Justin want to capture? *what snails look like, how they move*
  - What has Justin added using his imagination? *the blackbird*
  - What might Justin use these notes for? *as a story starter, to paint a picture, to write a poem*

- Justin used his notes to write a poem. Reveal the poem and read it aloud.

Word and sentence level work

1 Invite pupils to pick out the key words in the poem that are taken from the notes.

2 What words did Justin add to the poem? e.g. *shivering like snow, dialogue* Why do pupils think he did this?

Group activities: differentiation

Pupils work in pairs on **PCM 33**, picking out the key words in the text. **Higher attainers** can go on to pick out the words that are not essential to meaning.

Guided reading. Support **lower attainers** in picking out key words.

Plenary

Discuss which were the key words and why. Invite a few pupils to sum up as briefly as possible what the boy said about his friend.

YOU WILL NEED

- **OHT 18** – Notes and poem
- **PCM 33** – My Friend

ICT　For activities linked to this lesson see **PAGE 104**

HOMEWORK

Ask pupils to write some notes or a memo to themselves. It could be observational notes like Justin's, or a list or reminder, but it must have a real purpose.

Link to reading objective	
● To identify key words, phrases or sentences in reading.	3.2 T17

Assumed prior knowledge	
● Making simple notes.	2.3 T19
● Recording information.	3.1 T22

Planning suggestion

This unit can be used as part of a week focusing on notemaking. It can be linked to Unit 19, as part of an exploration of the different forms and purposes of notes.

LESSON TWO

SHARED WRITING

● Spend a few minutes discussing pupils' memos to themselves.

● Explain the lesson objective: *to practise making notes while someone is talking, to remember facts.*

● Pupils will be using their notes afterwards to write about each other.

● Explain that it's not easy to listen and write at the same time. There is only time to jot down a few words, so you have to pick out the important facts.

● Ask a talkative, confident pupil to start talking about themselves – their family, interests, likes and dislikes etc. Model taking notes as they talk, grouping the key facts under the appropriate headings.

● Stop after a few sentences to explain why you chose those key words. Use them to recall what the pupil said. Have you remembered the facts accurately?

● Look at the notes together. Will they make sense later on? Will you be able to use them to write a fuller description of the person?

● If necessary, continue the demonstration for another minute, so that pupils are clear about what they need to do.

Group activities: differentiation

Working in pairs, pupils take it in turns to tell their partner about themselves. Their partner makes notes, using **PCM 34** if they wish. Stop them half way through the session to swap roles.

Guided writing. Support **lower attainers** by working as a group, with one pupil talking while you scribe notes. Help them to delete uneccessary words.

Plenary

Discuss what pupils found easy and difficult about the task. Ask one or two to use their notes to talk to the class about their partner. How well did they recall the facts from their notes?

EXTENDED WRITING

Pupils use their notes to write a fuller description of their partner for a class book called 'Read All About Us'.

YOU WILL NEED

● **OHT 19** – Notemaking frame
● **PCM 34** – Notemaking frame

ICT For activities linked to this lesson see **PAGE 104**

WATCH OUT FOR

▶ Including unnecessary words: and, the etc.
▶ Writing too slowly.
▶ Difficulty in organising information logically.

MAIN WRITING OBJECTIVE

- **To describe and sequence key incidents by mapping.** 3.2 T7

Word and sentence level objective

- To infer the meaning of new words from context and generate a range of possible meanings. 3.2 W18

LESSON ONE

YOU WILL NEED

- **Pupil's Book** pages 34–35
- **OHT 19** – Journey map
- **PCM 35** – Journey map

MODEL TEXT

- Explain the lesson objective: *to look at an example of a story map.*

- A good way of remembering what happens in a story is to draw a map. Ask pupils if they know of any stories that include a map, e.g. *Winnie the Pooh, Goosey Farm, the Katy Morag stories, The Hobbit.*

- Look at the map of Loneland together. Explain that Jack's journey begins in Sunnybeck. Can pupils find it on the map? What does the arrow mean?

- Find Dragon Dread's Lair – this is where Jack is going.

- Read the story outline of Jack's Journey. Ask pupils to pick out some of the other places or features on the map. Can they spot where the will o' the wisps might live? *Will o' the Wisps Way*

- Discuss how the names of places give us clues to what they are like. What do pupils imagine the 'Mountains of Doom' and 'Forest Dire' to be like? Look at some other examples. What kind of place do they think Sunnybeck sounds like? How might it be different from Loneland?

Word and sentence level work

Ask pupils what dire, forsaken and perilous mean. Look the words up in a dictionary. Can pupils find any other gloomy words in the names of other places? *lone, shadow, black, doom*

Group activities: differentiation

In pairs, pupils use the story outline and the map on **PCM 35** to plan the route from Sunnybeck to Dragon Dread's Lair. **Higher attainers** could go on to show where some of the adventures might have happened.

Plenary

Ask pupils to present their maps. Discuss possible routes through Loneland using clues from the story outline.

ICT For activities linked to this lesson see **PAGE 104**

HOMEWORK

Ask pupils to make notes about a story which involves a journey, e.g. Little Red Riding Hood, or Hansel and Gretel. There could be adventures along the way.

Link to reading objective	
● To identify typical story themes.	3.2 T2

Assumed prior knowledge	
● To understand time and sequential relationships in stories.	2.1 T4
● Retelling stories.	2.2 T7
● Story settings.	2.2 T5

Planning suggestion

This unit can be used as part of extended work on planning and writing stories and links to other units on planning, setting and character.

LESSON TWO

SHARED WRITING

YOU WILL NEED
● Blank OHT or flipchart

- Remind pupils how story maps can help you to imagine where adventures happen.

- Explain the lesson objective: *to make their own story maps showing where the main events of a story they know well take place.*

- Ask pupils to suggest some examples of stories with a journey. Discuss which would be good ones for them to work on. Choose one to model in shared writing, or use Little Red Riding Hood as a simple example.

- Brainstorm ideas for the map by asking: What is the main setting for the story? Where does the character start and finish? Where do the events happen? What places or people are visited along the way?

- Draw a rough map as you go along, explaining that it will need to be revised and tidied up later.

- Model labelling the points on the map, and using arrows to show where the main events happen.

Group activities: differentiation

Pupils work in pairs to draw a map showing the key places and events of a short journey story. **Lower attainers** could continue the work from shared writing. **Higher attainers** could think of other adventures the characters might have and add new places to the map.

Guided writing. Help pupils to organise the main events and settings, and to place and label them clearly on the map.

Plenary

Look at work in progress. Are the maps clear? Discuss how pupils might draw maps about stories of their own. It could help them to plan the main events.

EXTENDED WRITING

Pupils practise telling their stories using their maps. They then revise and improve them and make a final copy.

ICT For activities linked to this lesson see **PAGE 104**

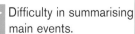

WATCH OUT FOR
▸ Difficulty in summarising main events.
▸ Muddled sequencing.

MAIN WRITING OBJECTIVE

- **To write instructional texts such as rules, using different organisational devices.**   3.2 T16

Word and sentence level objective

- To understand the differences between verbs in the 1st, 2nd and 3rd person; to use 2nd person for instructional texts.   3.2 S10

LESSON ONE

YOU WILL NEED
- **Pupil's Book** pages 36–37
- **PCM 36** – Rules

MODEL TEXT

- Explain the lesson objective: *to look at a range of simple rules.*

- Explain that *rules* are a form of instructions. Refer to school or class rules, and ask pupils to give the purpose of each.

- Ask two pupils to read through the rules for hamsters. After each rule is read ask pupils to give a reason for it, e.g. *don't chew electric wires in case you get electrocuted*

- Ask pupils to find the verbs in these rules. *chew, dig, eat, learn etc* Where do they appear? *at the beginning of each rule*

- Look at the Yo-yo rules. Ask pupils what the purpose of these rules is. *to make you play safely, prevent people being hurt* Which words tell you these are safety rules? *never, make sure, always*

- What is different about the way the hamster rules and the Yo-yo rules are set out? *hamster rules use sub-headings and bullet points; Yo-yo rules have a main heading and numbered points*

- Look at the rules for playing the Safari game. Ask pupils to read them through. Why are these rules important? *tell you how to play the game, make sure everyone knows what to do* What do these rules have that the others don't? *a 'You will need' box*

Word and sentence level work

1 Look at the Animal Safari rules. Ask pupils to pick out the pronouns and verbs in each rule, e.g. *If **you land** on 'Danger', **you miss** a turn.* Explain that this is the second person.

2 Re-write point 6 using the first and then the third person, e.g. If **I get** to the Safari Lodge first **I am** the winner. What words did you have to change? *verbs*

ICT For activities linked to this lesson see **PAGE 105**

Group activities: differentiation

PCM 36

All pupils use **PCM 36**. **Lower attainers** complete questions 1–3. If possible, offer support with question 3. **Higher attainers** do all the activities.

Plenary

Where might you find the yo-yo rules? Discuss who might have written the rules and why it is important to know.

Link to reading objectives

● To identify the different purposes of instructional texts, e.g. rules.	3.2 T12
● To understand how instructional texts are organised.	3.2 T14

Assumed prior knowledge

● To recognise different ways of presenting texts.	2.2 S7
● Grammatical agreement of verbs and nouns/pronouns.	2.2 S4
● Use of direct and impersonal writing.	2.1 T18

Planning suggestion

This unit can be used as part of a week looking at different forms of instructional writing.
It links to Unit 18.

LESSON TWO

SHARED WRITING

- Invite some pupils to share their rules written for homework. Discuss briefly the similarities and differences and the purpose of each.

- Explain the lesson objective: *to write a set of rules.*

- Display the picture of the Playground, and ask pupils to spot some of the safety hazards.

- Circle two of the hazards and ask pupils to say why they are dangerous. Make notes of useful words on the flipchart. Can they suggest a rule for each?

- Discuss the purpose and audience of the rule. *users of the playground, children and adults*

- With pupils, write out two rules on the board or flipchart. Which are the verbs? Put them at the beginning of the rule. Model using the second person.

- Show pupils how to edit the rules for clarity and conciseness.

- Discuss how you could set them out, using headings, bullet points or numbers. You could use the Must/Must not formula of the rules for hamsters, or you could make a list of Dos and Don'ts.

Group activities: differentiation

All pupils work in pairs to draft a set of rules for using the playground, referring to **PCM 37.**

Guided writing. Work with **lower attainers**. Help them to write clearly and to think about layout. Use the Must/Must not model.

Plenary

Invite pairs of pupils to read their work in progress. Others comment on the clarity of the language and the layout.

EXTENDED WRITING

Pupils revise and finish writing their rules and then illustrate them. They could include pictures of what **could** happen if the rules are not followed.

YOU WILL NEED

- **OHT 20** – Playground scene
- **PCM 37** – Playground scene
- Flipchart or board
- **Prompt Chart 5** – Rules and Instructions

ICT For activities linked to this lesson see **PAGE 105**

WATCH OUT FOR
- ▶ Over-use of personal pronouns.
- ▶ Unclear layout and spacing.

16

Too Much Searching

● TRADITIONAL TALE/PARABLE

MAIN WRITING OBJECTIVE

- **To write a story plan for a traditional tale, using story theme from reading but substituting different characters or changing the setting.** 3.2 T9

Word and sentence level objectives

- To investigate and identify basic rules for changing the spelling of nouns when s is added. 3.2 W9
- Singular and plural. 3.2 S4

LESSON ONE

MODEL TEXT

- Do pupils know what a parable is? *a story which teaches a lesson*

- Explain the lesson objective: *to look at an example of a traditional tale which teaches a lesson.*

- The parable of 'Too Much Searching' is a traditional tale from Africa. Read the story aloud, then ask pupils to summarise the main events. *man goes out to look for wood, moves rock, rock disturbs antelope, antelope disturbs buffalo, buffalo kills hunter, villagers find hunter*

- Ask pupils:
  – How did the villagers know that something was wrong? *the vultures hovering over the dead hunter*
  – How did they work out what had happened? *traced the footprints and marks on the ground; guessed that someone had moved the rock*
  – What lesson does this tale teach? *it's best to make use of what is near you, don't be fussy* Do you agree with this?

- Do pupils know what a proverb is? A proverb is a saying which gives advice. Make a list of a few proverbs on the board and explore their message, e.g. *no smoke without fire; a rolling stone gathers no moss; listeners hear no good of themselves; a bird in the hand is worth two in the bush*

- Ask the children to describe the pattern of the story. *it's like a cycle, a chain of events – one thing leads to another and then the events are unravelled*

Word and sentence level work

Teach the terms 'singular' and 'plural'. How would you normally make a noun plural? *add an s* Give some examples.
Look at the spelling of 'bushes' on line 9. Investigate whether nouns ending in -sh always use -es to make them plural.

Group activities: differentiation

Pupils work in pairs to complete the story chain on **PCM 38**.

Plenary

Ask selected pupils to retell the story from memory, using the story chain as a prompt. Reinforce the pattern.

YOU WILL NEED

- **Pupil's Book** pages 38–39
- **PCM 38** – Story chain
- **PCM 39** – Homework

ICT For activities linked to this lesson see **PAGE 105**

HOMEWORK

Pupils pluralise the nouns on **PCM 39** and try and identify some rules.

Link to reading objective	
● To investigate styles of traditional story language.	3.2 T1

Assumed prior knowledge	
● Traditional tales/parables.	
● Simple character descriptions.	2.2 T14
● Retelling stories.	2.2 T7

Planning suggestion

This unit can be used as part of extended work on story planning. It links to Unit 11 and to Unit 14. It can also be used to support work on traditional story characters, linked to Unit 12.

LESSON TWO

SHARED WRITING

- Remind pupils of the cycle of events in *Too Much Searching*, and that the story ended in a lesson.

- Explain the lesson objective: *to plan your own parable using* Too Much Searching *as a model.*

- You will be changing the characters, setting and events but it will teach the same lesson.

- Discuss how you might change the setting. Maybe you could set your parable in this country? Ask for suggestions.

- Discuss ideas for different characters. *children playing a ball game in a park, a family on holiday*

- Decide on an event that will start the story. *ball lands in someone's garden, dog chases cat across a road, a car goes out of control*

- Model using the story chain to help you map out the events. Show them how to make brief notes only. Remind pupils of the shape of the story – starts peacefully, one thing leads to another, causes chaos, leads to a climax and a lesson. Remember what the lesson needs to be – too much searching disturbs things that are still.

- Who is going to unravel the chain? *police officer? child? parent?*

Group activities: differentiation

Working in pairs, pupils plan their own parable using the story chain on **PCM 40** to help them. **Lower attainers** could continue with the work from shared writing. **Higher attainers** should rewrite the proverb in their own words.

Guided writing. Help **lower attainers** to focus on key events.

Plenary

Ask selected pairs to tell their story using the chain as a prompt.

EXTENDED WRITING

Pupils write the first draft of their parable, using the story chain to help them. As they revise their work, they should look out for plural spellings and check they are correct.

YOU WILL NEED

- **OHT 22** – Blank story chain
- **PCM 40** – Blank story chain

ICT For activities linked to this lesson see **PAGE 105**

WATCH OUT FOR

▶ Difficulty in following the chain pattern logically.
▶ Trying to write the whole story on the plan.

17

Mighty Mountain • SEQUEL

MAIN WRITING OBJECTIVE

- **To write alternative sequels to traditional stories using same characters and settings.**   3.2 T10

Word and sentence level objectives

- Capitalisation in names.   3.2 S8
- To explore opposites.   3.2 W24
- Adjectives.   3.2 S2

LESSON ONE

MODEL TEXT

- Ask pupils to think about the typical ingredients of a traditional tale. Encourage them to think about the characters, setting and plot.

- Display the **Prompt Chart** and discuss each feature. Explain that a traditional tale will have most of these ingredients.

- Explain the lesson objective: *to read a traditional tale and identify all the typical ingredients.*

- Read *Mighty Mountain* aloud. Identify some of the ingredients listed on the **Prompt Chart**:
  - Discuss the characters. Why are they typical? What typical adjectives are used? *biggest, strongest, pretty, old*
  - What is typical about the plot? *involves a journey/a quest*
  - What is typical about the events? *magical, superhuman, mysterious*
  - Are there any magic numbers? *3 women*

- Ask pupils to find examples of typical traditional tale language. Look at the opening in particular. *Many years ago . . . ; One warm autumn day . . .; They came at last . . .*

- Invent a typical ending for the tale, e.g. *From that day to this, Mighty Mountain never boasted again.*

Word and sentence level work

1 Ask pupils to find opposite adjectives in the story, e.g. *huge/tiny, big/small, young/old.* Think of some opposites for: *warm, pretty, strong, wrinkled.*

2 Recap rules for using capital letters. Ask the children to point out examples of capital letters used for names.

Group activities: differentiation

Leave the **Prompt Chart** clearly displayed, or give pupils copies. Working in pairs, pupils identify the typical traditional tale ingredients in the story and make notes on **PCM 41**. **Higher attainers** think of stories which include other features.

Plenary

Look at some completed ingredients charts. Discuss what Mighty Mountain might do next. Does he get to the wrestling match?

YOU WILL NEED

- **Pupil's Book** pages 41–42
- **Prompt Chart 6** – Traditional Tale Ingredients
- **PCM 41** – Ingredients chart

 ICT   For activities linked to this lesson see **PAGE 105**

HOMEWORK

What might happen next? Ask pupils to make notes. They could try and include some of the ingredients not used in the story so far.

- To investigate the styles and voices of traditional story language.　　3.2 T1

Assumed prior knowledge
- Traditional tales.
- Simple character descriptions.　　2.2 T14
- Retelling stories.　　2.2 T7
- To understand time and sequential relationships in stories.　　2.1 T4

Planning suggestion

This unit can be used as part of a week looking at the language and structure of traditional tales. It links to Unit 12 and Unit 16.

LESSON TWO

SHARED WRITING

- Quickly recap the story of Mighty Mountain.
- Explain the lesson objective: *to write a sequel to Mighty Mountain.*
- Explain that a sequel is a new story that follows on from the one before. It includes the same main characters but introduces new events and settings. Give some examples.
- Ask pupils to suggest what might happen next. Agree an outline story together. Jot down brief notes on the planner.
  - Perhaps Mighty Mountain has to pay a forfeit for being so vain – maybe cooking and cleaning for the three women.
  - Perhaps they agree to train him to be a better wrestler.
  - Maybe you could add a magic object as there wasn't one in the original, or even *three* magic objects, one from each woman.
- Brainstorm ideas for a new setting and different characters. Where does Mighty Mountain go? Who does he meet?
- Discuss a typical opening phrase for your story. *Many years later …; One fine spring morning…*
- Discuss possible endings. Think about traditional ones. Maybe Mighty Mountain marries Kuniko? Or maybe he saves his village?

Group activities: differentiation

Working in pairs, pupils use their homework notes to plan and draft a sequel to Mighty Mountain. **Lower attainers** could draw a storyboard instead.

Guided writing. Help pupils to use some of the language from the original to structure their writing and compose a suitable ending.

Plenary

Invite a pupil to read their sequel and explain how it will end. Evaluate the language and description. Does it sound like the original?

EXTENDED WRITING

Pupils revise their sequels, adding in more descriptive adjectives. They can then produce a final illustrated copy.

YOU WILL NEED
- **OHT 23** – Planning frame
- **Prompt Chart 6** – Traditional Tale Ingredients

ICT For activities linked to this lesson see **PAGE 105**

WATCH OUT FOR
- ▶ Difficulty in maintaining traditional language.
- ▶ Limited use of adjectives.
- ▶ Unsatisfactory endings.

18

How to ... ● INSTRUCTIONS

MAIN WRITING OBJECTIVE

● **To write instructions using a range of organisational devices.**   3.2 T16

Word and sentence level objective

● To note where commas occur in reading and to discuss their functions. 3.2 S6

LESSON ONE

MODEL TEXT

● Explain the lesson objective: *to look at different types of written instructions.*

● Read the instructions for recycling paper. Ask pupils:
  – Who are these instructions written for? *people wanting to recycle their own paper, probably children*
  – Why are the things you will need set out first, and in a list? *so you can see if you've got everything you need and get things ready first*
  – Why are the instructions divided into stages? *because you have to wait for things to happen in between*
  – What is the importance of the bullet points? *to separate different tasks; to give a clear order to what you need to do*
  – How do the pictures help? *show you more clearly what you have to do*

● Look at the recipe. What does it have in common with the instructions? *list of what you need, numbered instructions, pictures to help*

● Ask pupils to identify the verbs in each set of instructions, e.g. *rip, make, add* etc Where are they positioned? Why? *instructions start with a verb because verbs tell you what to do*

Word and sentence level work

1 Ask pupils to pick out the commas in the peanut butter recipe. How do they help the reader? *signal pauses, break up text*

2 Write out the 'You will need' section of Recycled Paper as one long sentence, e.g. *To make recycled paper, you will need some old paper, a bucket, some water ... etc* Which version is easier to follow, and why?

Group activities: differentiation

All pupils answer questions 1 and 2 on **PCM 42**, identifying the purpose and audience of the instructions, and answering questions about the recipe. **Higher attainers** should also do question 3.

Plenary

Invite pupils to say who they think each set of instructions is for. Instructions are usually written with a particular type of audience in mind and this affects how they are written.

YOU WILL NEED
● **Pupil's Book** pages 44–45
● **PCM 42** – Activities
● **PCM 43** – Homework

ICT For activities linked to this lesson see **PAGE 105**

HOMEWORK

Pupils use **PCM 43** to plan a set of instructions to show an alien how to clean his teeth. Remind them that they will need to be really clear! They could draw pictures if they want to.

Link to reading objectives

- To identify the different purposes of instructional texts, e.g. recipes etc. 3.2 T12
- How instructions are organised. 3.2 T14

Assumed prior knowledge

- Use of organisational devices to identify sequence and relationship. 2.1 S6
- To investigate and recognise a range of ways of presenting texts. 2.2 S7
- The function of verbs in sentences. 3.1 S3

Planning suggestion

This unit can be used as part of a week looking at instructional writing. Pupils can collect examples of instructions and explore the similarities and differences between the various forms. This unit links to Unit 15.

LESSON TWO

SHARED WRITING

- Spend a few minutes talking about the homework.
- Explain the lesson objective: *to write a set of instructions for an alien, for a book called* How to Survive on Earth.
- Brainstorm the skills an alien would need, e.g. *how to cross the road, how to make a cup of tea, how to catch a bus etc.*

- Choose one task to model. Remind pupils about the purpose and audience – you can't assume an alien knows anything, so the instructions will have to be really clear.
- Begin by making a list of all the things needed.
- Jot down all the things you need to do on a flipchart. Organise the points in to the right order.
- Write out the first few instructions. Ask pupils to suggest suitable verbs to start each sentence.
- Discuss any headings that will be helpful, and what pictures or diagrams could be added to make things even clearer.

Group activities: Differentiation

In pairs, pupils plan a set of instructions for the class book using **PCM 44** if needed. **Lower attainers** could continue the work from shared writing.

Guided writing. Ensure that pupils are clear about the audience and sequencing of the instructions. Work on features of layout that will help to make things clearer.

Plenary

Ask a couple of pairs to read their instructions aloud. Is each step clear? Are they in the right order? Would an alien understand it?

EXTENDED WRITING

Pupils finish writing their instructions, checking the order and clarity of their work, and adding any helpful drawings or diagrams.

They make a final copy for the class book *How to Survive on Earth: A Guide for Aliens.*

YOU WILL NEED

- **OHT 24** – Instruction Writing Frame
- **PCM 44** – Instruction Writing Frame
- Flipchart
- **Prompt Chart 5** – Rules an Instructions

 ICT For activities linked to this lesson see **PAGE 105**

 WATCH OUT FOR
- ▶ Unclear or out-of-sequence steps.
- ▶ Use of personal pronouns.

MAIN WRITING OBJECTIVE

- **To explore ways of writing ideas in shortened form e.g. notes, lists, headlines, messages; identifying purpose and audience.** 3.2 T17

Word and sentence level objective

- To experiment with deleting words in a sentence to see which are essential to meaning. 3.2 S9

LESSON ONE

MODEL TEXT

- Explain the lesson objective: *to look at some examples of notes and messages and to think about their audience and purpose.*

- Ask pupils to recall when they have sent or taken notes or messages. Why was each written and to whom was it sent?

- Look at the notes and messages together. Quickly summarise what each note is. *telephone message, note pinned to fridge, teacher's comments on work, reminder/to do list, headline*

- Read aloud the note for 'C'. Ask pupils:
  - Who is the message for and who is it from? *to C from his mum*
  - What is the main point of the message? *to give information; to say where mum is and when she'll be back, etc*
  - How is the message written? *list of facts, no punctuation, uses abbreviation*
  - Why is the message written in this way? *mum may have been in a hurry, needs to communicate key facts quickly*

- Read through the rest of the messages and discuss the same questions.

- Look at the newspaper headline. What does it have in common with the notes and messages. *uses abbreviated language, key words, not written in a sentence*

- Why do pupils think it is written this way? *headlines have to attract attention, need to say a lot in a few words*

Word and sentence level work

Write out the message to 'C' using sentences, e.g. *Craig, I have left a sandwich for you in the fridge.*
Identify the words that were added and discuss why they aren't needed in a note.

Group activities: differentiation

All pupils complete questions 1 and 2 on **PCM 45**. **Higher attainers** also write one or two sentences to explain the headline.

Plenary

Invite two pupils to read Dad's message as full sentences. How is it different from the note? Discuss the purpose of each of the messages.

YOU WILL NEED

- **Pupil's Book** pages 46–47
- **PCM 45** – Activities
- **PCM 46** – Homework

PB

PCM 45

ICT For activities linked to this lesson see **PAGE 106**

ICT For activities linked to this lesson see **PAGE 106**

HOMEWORK

Ask pupils to re-write the sentences on **PCM 46** as short messages.

Link to reading objective

- To discuss the purpose of notemaking and look at simple examples; to identify the intended audience.　　　3.2 T17

Assumed prior knowledge

- To make simple notes e.g. key words, headings.　　　2.3 T19
- To make a record of information listing key words.　　　3.1 T22

Planning suggestion

This unit can be used as part of a week looking at different forms of abbreviated writing and the purpose of making notes. It can be linked to Unit 13.

LESSON TWO

SHARED WRITING

- Spend a short time sharing pupils' homework, and reinforcing how to pick out the key words that are essential to meaning.

- Explain the lesson objective: *to make notes from a non-fiction text*.

- Display the OHT you have prepared. Ask a pupil to read it aloud. As they read, underline the key words in the text.

- With pupils' help, go back and make notes of the main ideas.

- Relate the notes to those read in the previous lesson. What do they have in common? *key points/facts, not in sentences*

- Explain that jotting down the main points in note form like this will help you to remember what you have read, or been told.

- What might you use these notes for? *to write a report about something* How does this effect what you will write? *you need to be able to remember the key facts, and you need to understand the notes when you look at them later on*

- Read another section of the book and ask pupils to make notes of the main points. Then ask them to feed back their ideas – have they captured all the key points? Is anything they have noted unecessary?

Group activities: differentiation

Give each group a copy of a text at their level of ability and ask pupils to make notes on one page or spread. The **lowest attainers** could continue with the text from shared writing. Remind them to capture the key points.

Guided writing. Work with **higher attainers** discussing how they might use their notes to write a report on the subject using their own words.

Plenary

Ask two groups to feed back the key points from their non-fiction text. Talk about the purpose of their notemaking. How might it be different if they wanted to write about only one aspect of the topic?

EXTENDED WRITING

Pupils finish making notes on their texts, then compare notes with a partner. Have they noted the same points? Pupils use their notes to rewrite the information in their own words.

YOU WILL NEED

- Selection of non-fiction texts relating to work in another subject
- OHT of a simple page from one of the texts

ICT For activities linked to this lesson see **PAGE 106**

WATCH OUT FOR

- The inclusion of unnecessary words.
- Copying out whole sentences.

20

The Hairy Toe • TRADITIONAL POEM

MAIN WRITING OBJECTIVE

- **To write new or extended verses for performance poetry, based on models using rhythm and repetition.** 3.2 T11

Word and sentence level objectives

- To infer the meaning of unknown words from context. 3.2 W18
- To write own definitions of words. 3.2 W20

LESSON ONE

MODEL TEXT

- Explain the lesson objective: *to read a traditional poem aloud and with expression.*

- Tell pupils the title of the poem. What kind of poem do they expect? *funny* Explain that it both is and isn't funny.

- This poem has no author. It is a traditional poem. Traditional poems are passed on orally.

- Read aloud 'The Hairy Toe'. Invite pupils to join in with the refrain.

- Emphasise the dramatic suspense and ghostly sound effects. The last line should be so loud that it makes everybody jump.

- What kind of creature do the children imagine? How would this creature speak? Try out various alternatives. Why are the words 'Hair-r-ry To-o-e' written as they are? *to make them long drawn out sounds, spooky*

- How might its voice sound different each time? Look for clues in the poem. *away off in the distance; the voice had come nearer etc*

- Where else might they add some special effects? *the wind moaning and groaning; the house creaking and cracking*

- How could they make these sounds? *percussion instruments; using their hands and feet*

Word and sentence level work

Ask pupils to point to any words they don't know the meaning of. What might 'scrooched' and 'smoosh' mean. Explain that they are made-up words which aren't in the dictionary. Work out some definitions together.

Group activities: differentiation

Pupils work in mixed ability groups to practise reading the poem aloud in preparation for performance. Encourage them to add sound effects where appropriate.

Guided reading. Work on performance and creating different effects by making your voice soft or loud.

Plenary

Listen to group performances and evaluate.

YOU WILL NEED

- Percussion instruments
- PCM 47 – Homework

 ICT For activities linked to this lesson see **PAGE 106**

HOMEWORK

Pupils imagine what the creature looks like, and draw and label a picture using **PCM 47**. They then think about how it might have lost its toe!

Link to reading objectives

- To choose and prepare poems for performance, identifying appropriate expression, tone, volume and use of voices and other sounds. **3.2 T4**
- To rehearse and improve performance. **3.2 T5**

Assumed prior knowledge

- Experience of reading poetry aloud.
- Poems with repeated phrases. **3.1 T13**

Planning suggestion

This unit could link to the study of traditional tales (Units 12, 16 and 17) exploring a different form of storytelling. Or you could focus on spooky poems, e.g. Colin McNaughton's 'There're an Awful Lot of Weirdos in our Neighbourhood'.

LESSON TWO

SHARED WRITING

- Explain the lesson objective: *to write some extra lines for The Hairy Toe, describing what happens next.*

- Ask pupils to share their drawings and ideas about how the creature lost its toe. What does the creature look like? Is it mean and nasty or small and sweet? This will effect what happens.

- Brainstorm what will happen next.
  – Where might the woman have put the hairy toe?
  – What will the creature do? Will it drag the woman away?
  – What will the woman do? Will she see the creature? How will she react?

- Start to compose some extra lines, using the writing frame if you wish. Include a description of the creature. Demonstrate how to use repeated phrases about its eyes, hands and feet. You could invent some words like 'scrooched'.

- Discuss the importance of creating atmosphere. Think of words that create good sounds. How could you write them to show how they should be said?

- What will the creature say when it gets its toe back? Write the lines together.

Group activities: differentiation

Pupils work in pairs to write extra lines for the poem, reading aloud as they go and thinking about sounds. **Lower attainers** can use **PCM 48** for support.

Guided writing. Focus on words that create sound. Discuss how they should be written. Help pupils to make words up if they want to.

Plenary

Invite pupils to read their drafts as dramatically as possible. How could they be improved?

EXTENDED WRITING

Pupils finish their extra lines or verses and then write out and illustrate a final version for a class display.

YOU WILL NEED

- **Pupil's Book** pages 48-49
- **OHT 25** – Writing frame
- **PCM 48** – Writing frame

ICT For activities linked to this lesson see **PAGE 106**

WATCH OUT FOR

► Difficulty in reflecting the features of the original poem.

21

Sea World ● SUMMARY

MAIN WRITING OBJECTIVE

● **To summarise in writing the content or main point of a passage.**   3.3 T26

Word and sentence level objective

● To identify and understand pronouns; substituting pronouns for nouns.   3.3 S2

LESSON ONE

MODEL TEXT

- Remind pupils of work they have done so far on notemaking. What is meant by the main idea of a piece of text? How would they pick out the key points?

- Explain the lesson objective: *to read a few short passages about the sea, and then say what the main point of each passage is.*

- Read the first paragraph aloud. Give pupils two minutes to talk about it and to think of a way to tell others the main point.

- Take general ideas first, e.g. *Most of the Earth's surface is covered by water.*

- Explain that this is a summary of the content of the paragraph. What key words does it include? *Earth, water*

- Read aloud the second paragraph. What is the main point of this paragraph? *to explain why the sea is salty*

- Ask a pupil to say why the sea is salty in as few words as possible. *because the water washes salt from rocks into the sea*

- Invite pupils to read aloud the third paragraph. What are the key words? *waves, tides, moving*

- How could you summarise the passage in one sentence? Use the key words, e.g. *Waves and tides keep the sea moving all the time.*

Word and sentence level work

Remind pupils how pronouns can be used to avoid the boring repetition of nouns in texts. Ask pupils to identify any pronouns in the text. Then discuss what they refer to, e.g. *our, these, they, it.*

Group activities: differentiation

Working in groups, pupils read paragraphs 4 and 5 about the sea and summarise them orally. **Higher attainers** should go on to summarise paragraph 6.

Guided reading. Help **lower attainers** to pick out the key words.

Plenary

Ask pupils from different groups to summarise the main point of each paragraph. Others should comment on whether the main point has been made adequately.

YOU WILL NEED

- **Pupil's Book** pages 51–52
- **OHT 26** – Sea World
- **PCM 49** – Homework

ICT For activities linked to this lesson see **PAGE 106**

HOMEWORK

Pupils complete the pronouns exercise on **PCM 49**.

Link to reading objective

- To summarise orally in one sentence the content of a passage or text, and the main point it is making.   3.3 T19

Assumed prior knowledge

- Writing in sentences.   3.1 S11
- To understand the need for grammatical agreement.   3.2 S11
- To make notes and identify purpose.   3.2 T17
- To note where commas occur in reading.   3.2 S6

Planning suggestion

The work in this unit should be related to work on a class topic. Pupils can go on to make a summary in note form of a longer text. They can then use their summaries to give an oral report on the topic.

LESSON TWO

SHARED WRITING

- Explain the lesson objective: *to write a short summary of a piece called 'Creatures of the Deep'.*
- Invite a confident pupil to read the first paragraph of 'Creatures of the Deep'. Ask others to pick out the key words and phrases. *deepest parts of the sea, no light/darkness, creatures, food, hunt*
- What is the paragraph about? *how creatures live in the dark depths of the sea*
- Discuss how you could summarise this paragraph in just one sentence. Remind pupils that they need to include only the main points. Compose the sentence together. Make sure it is both short and clear.
- Does it cover all the main points?
- Discuss the reasons for leaving certain information out.
- Read the rest of the text aloud, and explain that pupils will be summarising this in their groups.

Group activities: differentiation

Pupils work in groups to write summaries of the text on **PCM 50**. **Lower attainers** can do just paragraph 2.

Guided writing. Help pupils to pick out the main points, and to use pronouns where appropriate when writing their summaries.

Plenary

Invite a pupil from each group to read aloud their written summaries. How concise is it? Are the main points covered?

EXTENDED WRITING

Pupils read the whole piece about 'Sea World' in their books, and then write a summary using no more than 50 words.

YOU WILL NEED

- **OHT 27** – Creatures of the Deep
- Flipchart
- **PCM 50** – Creatures of the Deep

ICT   For activities linked to this lesson see **PAGE 106**

WATCH OUT FOR

▶ Listing of key words only.
▶ Over-use of 'and'.
▶ Copying out chunks of the passage.

22

The Market Street Mystery

● RECOUNT

MAIN WRITING OBJECTIVE

- **To recount the same event in a variety of ways, e.g. letter, news report.**   3.3 T22

Word and sentence level objective

- To use the apostrophe to spell contracted forms of words.   3.3 W11

LESSON ONE

MODEL TEXT

YOU WILL NEED
- **Pupil's Book** pages 54–55
- **PCM 51** – Features chart
- **PCM 52** – Homework

- Explain the lesson objective: *to look at different ways of recounting the same event.*

- Ask pupils to glance at the two pieces of writing in their books.
  - What forms of writing can they see? *a newspaper report, a letter*
  - How do they know, just by looking, what they are? *news report has a headline, letter has an address and signature*

- Explain that both these pieces of writing recount the same event. Read the news report aloud. Ask pupils:
  - Why has the school been closed? *strange smell, people feeling ill*
  - How does the parent feel about the school closing? Ask pupils to find the speech and to pick out the exact words. *not happy, something's got to be done*
  - Who wrote this news report? *Gerald Williams*
  - Why do you think he has included a direct quote from a parent? *real feelings of people involved, public interest, more personal*
  - What other people might the reporter have interviewed? Look for clues in the text. *children and teachers at the school – 'they all reported'; 'experts say'*

- Now read the letter. Who and has written this letter and why?

- Look at each paragraph of the letter and summarise what it does.

Word and sentence level work

1 Look for apostrophes used for contracted words in the news report. *I'm, something's.* Which words have been shortened?

2 Explore words which could be contracted in the letter. *it is, they cannot, there has* Discuss why they are not contracted.

For activities linked to this lesson see **PAGE 106**

Group activities: differentiation

Pupils work in groups to complete the activity on **PCM 51**. **Higher attainers** should go on to question 2, identifying the intended readership of the different pieces.

Plenary

Ask pupils to say where they found each feature. Talk about who might read each piece and how that affects the way they are written.

HOMEWORK

Pupils complete the exercise on **PCM 52**, extending and contracting words using apostrophes.
You may wish to read through it with them first.

Link to reading objective

- To read examples of letters written for a range of purposes e.g. to recount.   3.3 T16

Assumed prior knowledge

- To write simple reports from known information.   3.1 T23
- To notice differences in the style and structure of fact and fiction.   3.1 T18
- The basic conventions of speech punctuation.   3.1 S7

Planning suggestion

This unit can be used as part of a week looking at different ways of presenting the same information. Pupils could recount events through stories as well as exploring letters and news reports.

LESSON TWO

SHARED WRITING

- Discuss the homework. Remind pupils that words are usually shortened in speech, or in informal writing.

- Explain the lesson objective: *to write about a shared event in different ways.*

- Spend a few minutes discussing a recent shared event, such as a visit or a sports day. What happened? Who was there? What was special about it?

- Begin by modelling a letter. Who could they write to about the event? How will the choice of reader affect the language you use?

- Model writing the opening address, e.g. 'Dear Mr . . .', or 'Hi Sam!' How will the letter start? Think about the reader and the reason for writing. Write the first couple of sentences together.

- Now discuss how you would recount the event as a newspaper report. What different features will you need? *e.g. headline, quotes etc.* Ask pupils to suggest a headline.

- Model the opening paragraph. Introduce the events.

- Discuss where pupils could get quotes from for their article. Talk about some of the questions you could ask.

Group activities: differentiation

Pupils plan a recount of the shared event either as a news report or a letter. They can use the writing frames provided on **PCMS 53** and **54**.

Guided writing. Work with pupils who are planning a letter. Make sure they are clear about their audience and purpose and the style of language they need to use.

Plenary

Invite pupils to read or talk about their work in progress. Allow others to suggest further ideas and to say which bits sound good.

EXTENDED WRITING

Pupils finish writing their letter or news report, and read it to a partner, who checks that it is the right style for the type of writing. They then make changes and check spelling and punctuation.

YOU WILL NEED

- **OHT 28** – Letter writing frame
- **OHT 29** – News report writing frame
- **PCM 53** – Letter writing frame
- **PCM 54** – News report writing frame

 ICT For activities linked to this lesson see **PAGE 106**

WATCH OUT FOR

▸ Inappropriate language style.
▸ Changing tenses.
▸ Lack of awareness of audience and purpose.

23

Diary of a Killer Cat • FIRST PERSON

MAIN WRITING OBJECTIVE

- **To write a first person account, e.g. a character's own account of events in a story.**   3.3 T12

Word and sentence level objectives

- Pronouns: 1st, 2nd and 3rd person.   3.3 S2
- Grammatical agreement between pronouns and verbs.   3.3 S3

LESSON ONE

MODEL TEXT

- Recap the difference between 1st, 2nd and 3rd person. Discuss their different purposes in writing – 1st person for letters, recounts, and stories about yourself; 2nd person for instructions; 3rd person for writing about someone else.

- Explain the lesson objective: *to look at a story written in the first person and change it to the third person.*

- Read the extract from *The Diary of a Killer Cat*. Ask pupils:
  - Who is the 1st person telling the story? *the cat, Tuffy*
  - Is Tuffy sorry about killing the bird? Why do you think that? Which words tell us how he feels? *'I'm a cat. It's practically my job . . .'; 'it practically landed on my paws'*
  - How does Tuffy feel about Ellie? *she's making a big fuss, she doesn't understand cats*
  - What does Ellie think about Tuffy? What's the clue? *she cries but speaks lovingly; loves him but hates him killing things*

- How would the story sound if it was written in the 3rd person. *Once there was a killer cat called Tuffy …*

Word and sentence level work

1 Who does 'it' refer to in line 6? How do you know? *the bird – 'mouth' wouldn't make sense* Who is 'me' in line 8? And 'she' in line 10? Explain that these words are **pronouns**. They are useful in cutting out repetition.

2 Which words would you have to change to write the account in the third person? What would you write instead? *I – he/she/they; me – him/her/them; my – his/her/their*

Group activities: differentiation

Pupils work in pairs to write a 3rd person account of what happened. **Lower attainers** can use **PCM 55** for support.

Guided reading. Investigate instances when you can't replace a noun with a pronoun because of ambiguity.

Plenary

Ask individuals to read their 3rd person accounts. How does it change the story?

YOU WILL NEED

- **Pupil's Book** page 56
- **PCM 55** – Writing frame
- **PCM 56** – Homework: pronouns

ICT   For activities linked to this lesson see **PAGE 107**

HOMEWORK

Pupils complete the exercise on pronouns on **PCM 56**.

Link to reading objective

- To distinguish between 1st and 3rd person accounts.   3.3 T3

Assumed prior knowledge

- 1st and 3rd person.   3.2 S10
- Diary writing

Planning suggestion

This unit can be used to look at and compare writing 1st and 3rd person accounts. You could read the whole of *The Diary of a Killer Cat* or pupils could continue writing Jake's diary.

LESSON TWO

SHARED WRITING

- Remind pupils of yesterday's text, *Diary of a Killer Cat*. In which person was it written?

- Explain the lesson objective: *to look at a story written in the 3rd person and change it into a 1st person account.*

- Read 'Jake in Trouble' together. What is happening in the story? What kind of character is Jake? How does he feel about going to the farm? *looking forward to it, confident, excited, will miss his friends*

- Ask pupils to imagine Jake is writing a diary. What things would he write about? Underline them on the OHT.

- Model changing the opening sentence into the 1st person. Show pupils how to use a chatty style, e.g. *Hey, I'm so excited today. I'm going on holiday! Can you believe it? I'm going to a farm.*

- Encourage pupils to add their own ideas as well as using the text. Show them how they might do this. *I'm hoping that a farm is like a great big park, but I don't know because I've never seen one before.*

- Remind them about using pronouns and ask them to point one or two out. Jake won't be a 'he' in their writing. What will he be? Why?

Group activities: differentiation

Pupils use the text (provided on **PCM 57**) to write an entry for Jake's diary. **Lower attainers** can use the writing frame on **PCM 58**. **Higher attainers** can write the next entry, describing Jake's journey to the farm.

Guided writing. Comment on the use of pronouns, checking verb agreement. Encourage pupils to use a chatty style.

Plenary

Invite pupils to read their work in progress. Is the use of the 1st person consistent? Does it sound chatty?

EXTENDED WRITING

Pupils can write further entries for Jake's diary, inventing some new adventures for him.

YOU WILL NEED

- **OHT 30** – Jake in Trouble
- **PCM 57** – Jake in Trouble
- **PCM 58** – Jake's diary writing frame

ICT   For activities linked to this lesson see **PAGE 107**

WATCH OUT FOR

- Problems in maintaining first person.
- Difficulty in capturing chatty diary style.
- Over-use of pronouns.

24

May We Recommend • BOOK REVIEW

MAIN WRITING OBJECTIVE

- **To write book reviews for a specified audience.** 3.3 T14

Word and sentence level objective

- To collect new words and use them in own writing. 3.3 W12

LESSON ONE

YOU WILL NEED

- **Pupil's Book** page 58
- **PCM 59** – Review chart
- **PCM 60** – Homework

MODEL TEXT

- How do pupils choose what books to read? Have pupils ever had a book recommended to them by someone?

- Discuss other ways in which books can be recommended. *displays in bookshops or libraries, reviews in magazines, on TV or radio*

- Read aloud the book reviews written by Narina and Tom. Ask pupils:
  - What does Narina like about the book she has chosen? *makes her laugh*
  - Who does she recommend it to? *people who like animals*
  - What kind of book is Tom's review about? *non-fiction*
  - Does he think it is good? Why? *yes, because it tells you lots of interesting things and has good pictures*
  - What did Tom think was the best part? *how spiders catch big prey*
  - Who does Tom recommend the book to? *people who like science*
  - Who does he think might not like this book? *people who are scared of spiders*

- Ask if anyone has read either of these books. Do they agree with the reviewers? Why or why not? If they haven't read the books, do the reviews persuade them that the book is worth reading?

- Do the reviews say enough? What else would pupils want to know? *the genre, how easy or difficult the book is to read, what age it is for*

Word and sentence level work

1 Ask pupils to guess what 'recommend' means, then look it up in a dictionary.

2 Discuss other terminology that will be useful in writing a book review. *author, illustrator, plot, characters, setting, genre, facts etc.*

Group activities: differentiation

Pupils work in pairs to read and evaluate the reviews using **PCM 59**. **Lower attainers** could evaluate just one book.

Plenary

Take a vote on the best review. Point out that a review shouldn't give too much away, especially with a story!

ICT For activities linked to this lesson see **PAGE 107**

HOMEWORK

Pupils write about a book they have read recently using **PCM 60**.

Link to reading objective

- To be aware of authors and to discuss preferences and reasons for these.   3.3 T9

Assumed prior knowledge

- Comparing and evaluating books by different authors.   2.3 T7
- To express views about stories and poems.   3.1 T8
- Genre.

Planning suggestion

This unit can be used as part of a week studying a particular or favourite author. You could discuss and compare a range of books by the same author. You could follow up with Unit 26 and write a letter to the author.

LESSON TWO

SHARED WRITING

- Look briefly at the homework. Did anyone choose the same book? Were their opinions similar or very different?

- Explain the lesson objective: *to write book reviews for a display in the school library.*

- Choose a story or a non-fiction book that the class have recently read. Discuss who will read the review (other pupils and teachers) and why it is important to know this before you start writing.

- Use one of the writing frames to help you model the review.

- If you're working on a story: What you would say about the setting and main characters? Ask pupils to sum up the plot in two sentences – remind them not to give too much away!

- If you are working on non-fiction: help pupils to summarise what the book is about and to comment on the layout and illustrations. Is the book easy to read? Is it interesting?

- Ask pupils to suggest something they really liked about the book. Or perhaps they disliked it. How would this change the review?

- End with a recommendation. Who might enjoy reading it?

Group activities: differentiation

Pupils work in pairs or on their own to write book reviews. You may need to supply copies of books they have read, or to remind them of details such as title and author. **Lower attainers** could just make notes on **PCM 63** or **64**.

Guided writing. Help pupils to say precisely why they liked a particular book, and to think about who might also enjoy reading it.

Plenary

Invite pupils to read out their reviews. Do they make others want to read the book?

EXTENDED WRITING

Pupils finish writing their reviews and present for the library display. They could write a second review of another type of writing.

YOU WILL NEED

- **OHT 31** – Fiction review frame
- **OHT 32** – Non-fiction review frame
- **PCM 61** – Fiction review frame
- **PCM 62** –Non-fiction review frame

ICT For activities linked to this lesson see **PAGE 107**

WATCH OUT FOR
- Difficulty in summarising plot.
- Vague reasons for choice: 'it was good'.

25

Dear Author ● LETTER

MAIN WRITING OBJECTIVE

- **To write letters to authors about books.**   3.3 T20
- **To organise letters in to simple paragraphs.**   3.3 T23

Word and sentence level objective

- To use conjunctions to write more complex sentences.   3.3 S5

LESSON ONE

YOU WILL NEED

- **Pupil's Book** pages 60–61
- **PCM 63** – Apology letter

MODEL TEXT

- Explain the lesson objective: *to look at the language and presentation of letters written for different purposes.*

- Spend a few minutes talking about different reasons for writing a letter. *telling a friend about something, thanking someone, asking for information, saying sorry*

- Ask pupils if they know any rules for setting out letters.

- Look at the selection of letters together. Who wrote them? What is the purpose of each one? *to ask for a catalogue; letter to an author; to thank someone; to say hi to friends*

- Ask pupils to comment on the different layouts.
  – Why has Nicki just put 'Chalk Cottage' as her address? Why has Lee given no address at all? *they are writing to friends and relatives who probably know where they live*
  – Why has Francesca not written an address? *letterhead paper*

- Look at the different openings and endings of the letters. Which are formal and which are informal?

- Ask pupils to pick out examples of chatty language *Hi guys!* and more formal language *I am writing to ask …*

Word and sentence level work

1 Look at some of the connectives used by Francesca to make her sentences longer, e.g *because, and, especially*

2 Read Lee's letter again. Discuss how you could join some of the sentences together to make it flow better. Write out a couple of examples, e.g. *I've got some new friends but I really miss you all.*

Group activities: differentiation

Working in pairs pupils look at the letter on **PCM 63** and identify the purpose and style. **Higher attainers** write a letter to a friend telling them what happened.

Plenary

Ask pupils the purpose of the letter. Pick out some formal features. Invite one or two pupils to read out the letter to a friend.

ICT For activities linked to this lesson see **PAGE 107**

HOMEWORK

Ask pupils to make notes about a favourite author ready for writing a fan letter. They should include titles of favourite books, favourite bits and some questions to ask.

Link to reading objective
- To read examples of letters written for a range of purposes; to look at ways of addressing different audiences.   3.3 T16

Assumed prior knowledge
- To express views about a story.   3.1 T8
- To compare and evaluate books by different authors.   2.3 T7

Planning suggestion

This unit can be used as part of a week looking at letters written for different purposes. It can also be linked to the book reviews in Unit 24.

LESSON TWO

SHARED WRITING

- Explain the objective: *to write a letter to a favourite author.*
- Share the homework and make a list of favourite authors.
- What could you include in a fan letter? What is likely to persuade somebody to reply? *good detail, thoughtful comments about their books, polite language, neat presentation, interesting questions*
- Write a list of possible questions on the board. What do pupils want to know about the authors? e.g. *What is your favourite book? Did you like reading when you were at school?* Encourage them to ask questions about how they work. e.g. *Where do you get your ideas? How long does it take you to write? How do you get started?*
- Choose one popular author to model a letter to, explaining that pupils can choose their own author when they do their own writing. Demonstrate where to write the address and first line.
- Discuss sequencing the letter in paragraphs. Start by giving your reason for writing, then talk about your favourite books – describe the best bits and why you like them. Finish by asking two or three questions. Don't ask too many!
- Show pupils how to sign off the letter.

Group activities: differentiation

Pupils work on their own, writing a letter to their favourite author or poet. **Lower attainers** can use **PCM 64** for support, but encourage them to change it to suit their own needs.

Guided writing. Focus on sequencing the letter in paragraphs, and using connectives to write longer sentences.

Plenary

Read and discuss some of the letters. How could they be improved?

EXTENDED WRITING

Pupils finish and revise their letters. They can then make a final copy to send to the author. Alternatively, you could see if the author has their own website and contact them by e-mail.

YOU WILL NEED

- **OHT 33** – Letter writing frame
- **PCM 64** – Letter writing frame

ICT For activities linked to this lesson see **PAGE 107**

WATCH OUT FOR
▶ Difficulty in organising the letter into paragraphs.

MAIN WRITING OBJECTIVE

- **To plot a sequence of episodes modelled on a known story.**   3.3 T10
- **To write extended stories based on a plan, set out in simple chapters.**   3.3 T13

Word and sentence level objective

- To investigate how words and phrases can signal time sequence.   3.3 S6

LESSON ONE

MODEL TEXT

- Explain the lesson objective: *to look at a story planned using simple chapters.*

- A Year 3 class noticed leaking pipes near their school. They used the idea to plan a story about a flood.

- Read aloud Chapter 1 of 'Flood!' Ask pupils:
  – Who are the main characters in this story? *Sam, Steve and Jamie*
  – Where is the story set? *in their school*
  – What happens in this first chapter? *water bursts from the roadworks and starts a flood; children run to school, they are trapped*
  – Why do you think the writers stopped the first chapter where the head tells everybody they're marooned? *dramatic, cliffhanger*

- Read aloud Chapter 2. Ask pupils:
  – How is the plot developed? Summarise the key events. *children are waiting for their lunch, they notice the water is rising, water starts to creep into the school and they are frightened*
  – What does the first paragraph of the chapter do? *shows how time has moved on – to lunchtime*
  – What does the second paragraph do? *reintroduces the flood*

- Recap what these first two chapters do – Chapter 1 sets the scene, introduces characters and opens the plot; Chapter 2 develops the plot a bit more.

Word and sentence level work

1 Ask pupils to find words and phrases that show the passage of time. *waterworks ... for over a month, the next day, meanwhile, suddenly*

2 Discuss how useful these phrases are in building up a story. Think of other examples. *later that day, the very next night, many years later*

Group activities: differentiation

Working in groups, pupils discuss what might happen next in the story, then add the main points to the chapter plan on **PCM 65**. **Higher attainers** could think of cliffhanger endings for each of their chapters.

Plenary

Ask pupils to share their plans for the remaining chapters. Discuss which ideas would work best and why.

YOU WILL NEED
- **Pupil's Book** pages 62–63
- **PCM 65** – Chapter plan
- **PCM 66** – Homework

  For activities linked to this lesson see **PAGE 108**

HOMEWORK

Pupils think about a story of their own, based on the idea of being trapped in school. It could be by a flood, or they could think of something else. Ask them to brainstorm ideas for the characters, setting and plot, and to make brief notes on **PCM 66**.

Link to reading objective

- To refer to significant aspects of the text.   3.3 T2

Assumed prior knowledge

- Story settings.   3.1 T11
- Planning the main points of a story.   3.2 T6

Planning suggestion

This unit, together with Unit 27, provides a whole week's work looking at planning a story in simple chapters and using paragraphs to organise plot and dialogue.

LESSON TWO

SHARED WRITING

- Explain the lesson objective: *to plan their own chapter stories called 'Trapped!' based on 'Flood!'.*

- Start with a general brainstorm, using pupils' homework ideas.
  - Who might the story be about and where is it set?
  - Why are the children trapped? *infectious disease, siege, plague of insects*
  - What is going to happen? *they might be trapped for weeks, they might run out of food or water, they might send someone to get help*
  - How will it end? *perhaps the head teacher saves the day, or one of the pupil's parents braves the danger to come and rescue them*

- Start to plan out the story using the chapter frame.

- Remind pupils of the purpose of the opening chapter – they need to set the scene and introduce the characters and events.

- What will happen next? Make notes for the middle of the story. Help pupils to think about how to build the events up to a climax. Think about signalling time sequences. Change the chapter headings if necessary to suit your own story.

- How will the story end? Remind them that they need to tie up any loose ends. The ending is important and they shouldn't rush it just to get the story finished.

Group activities: differentiation

Pupils work in pairs to plan their own chapter stories using **PCM 67**. **Lower attainers** can continue with the ideas from shared writing. **Higher attainers** should be encouraged to write their own chapter headings.

Guided writing. Help pupils to build a logical sequence into their story plans. Discuss the function of each of the chapters.

Plenary

Invite pairs to share their story plans. Does each chapter have a clear purpose? Is the build up clear? Does the ending work?

EXTENDED WRITING

The extended writing exercise is incorporated in the work of Unit 27, where pupils will be looking more closely at the detail of their stories. Pupils can finish and revise their plans if necessary.

YOU WILL NEED

- **OHT 34** – Chapter planning frame
- Flipchart
- **PCM 67** – Chapter planning frame
- **Prompt Chart 1** – Story Writing

For activities linked to this lesson see **PAGE 108**

WATCH OUT FOR
- Lack of logical sequence.
- Writing out the story on the planning sheet.

MAIN WRITING OBJECTIVES

- **To write openings to stories or chapters; to use language to build up tension, create moods, set scenes.**   3.3 T11
- **To write extended stories based on a plan, set out in simple chapters and using paragraphs to organise.**   3.3 T13

Word and sentence level objective

- To use speech marks and other dialogue punctuation.   3.3 S4

LESSON ONE

YOU WILL NEED

- **Pupil's Book** pages 62–63
- **PCM 68** – Chapter 2
- **PCM 69** – Homework

MODEL TEXT

- Explain the lesson objective: *to explore how language is used in stories to create effect.*

- Remind pupils of the story they have been looking at called 'Flood!'. You are going to look at the structure and language in more detail.

- Read Chapter 1 aloud. Ask pupils to recap the purpose of an opening chapter. *set the scene, introduce character, start off the plot*

- Look at the first few paragraphs, including the opening dialogue. How does this set the scene? What mood does it create? *the boys are fed up, bored, they are wondering how much longer it can go on*

- Are there any bits of the opening that don't work so well? *repetition of 'wondered', too many characters?*

- How does the language change in the next paragraph? Ask pupils to identify specific words and phrases, e.g. *suddenly, "help!", pouring, ran for their lives* What effect does this have? *adds excitement, drama, suspense*

- Look at the last paragraph of the chapter. What is good about it? *it sets up the story, ends on a cliffhanger* What is not so good about it? *it's a bit abrupt, skips quite a lot of time, language isn't very dramatic*

- What could you do to improve it? *add verbs, adverbs, adjectives*

Word and sentence level work

Ask pupils to identify examples of dialogue, and use the text to revise speech punctuation, particularly the use of a new paragraph for a new speaker.

ICT For activities linked to this lesson see **PAGE 108**

Group activities: differentiation

Working in pairs, pupils look at Chapter 2 on **PCM 68** and discuss what Jakk and Ranjit could improve. **Higher attainers** can think of some alternatives for 'wondered', 'sighed' and 'suddenly'.

Guided reading. Help **lower attainers** to evaluate the story. Which bits are not important? Which bits need to be explained?

HOMEWORK

PCM 69 is a copy of Chapter 1, with no dialogue punctuation or paragraphs. Pupils should add in the speech marks and other punctuation, and indicate where new paragraphs are needed.

Plenary

Ask pupils to suggest improvements to the story. Comment on their ideas. Explain that this is why it is important to revise your work.

Link to reading objective

● To refer to significant aspects of the text.	3.3 T2

Assumed prior knowledge

● The basic conventions of speech punctuation.	3.1 S7
● How paragraphs are used to organise dialogue.	3.1 T2
● To begin to organise stories in paragraphs.	3.1 T16

Planning suggestion

This unit can be used as part of a week looking at planning and writing stories in chapters. It continues the work of Unit 26, focusing on the chapter content in more detail and exploring the use of language to create effect.

LESSON TWO

SHARED WRITING

● Explain the lesson objective: *to begin to write the story they have planned called 'Trapped!'.*

● Ask pupils to refer back to the stories they planned based on 'Flood!'. Recap some of their ideas.

● Use one of the plans to base the shared writing on, choosing a chapter to model writing with the class.

● Ask pupils to recap how paragraphs are used to build up tension in stories. They move the story on, and signal changes in events or atmosphere.

● Make notes for each paragraph. Can pupils suggest some cliffhanger endings?

● Take more detailed ideas for the opening paragraph – setting the scene. Encourage pupils to think about using language to create a particular effect. Write the paragraph together on the flipchart, showing pupils how to add effective details and to think about the best words to use as you go along.

● If you have time, draft another paragraph with pupils. Try to include some dialogue, reviewing the rules for setting it out.

Group activities: differentiation

Pupils work in pairs, using the plans they made for Unit 26 as the basis for their story writing. They should draft at least one chapter together, using the frame on **PCM 70** if necessary.

Guided writing. Support **lower attainers** by scribing a chapter with them. Show them how to make the language interesting.

Plenary

Invite pupils to read out the chapters they have written. Comment on the language and the effective use of paragraphs.

EXTENDED WRITING

Pupils finish drafting their stories. They could divide the story up and write two more chapters each. If possible, allow time for pupils to revise their stories before producing a final version.

YOU WILL NEED

● **OHT 35** – Chapter writing frame
● Completed story plans from Unit 26
● **PCM 70** – Chapter writing frame
● Flipchart

For activities linked to this lesson see **PAGE 108**

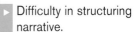

WATCH OUT FOR
▶ Difficulty in structuring narrative.
▶ Lack of tension or action.
▶ Too much description.

The Sound Collector
● ONOMATOPOEIA

MAIN WRITING OBJECTIVE

- **To write poetry that uses sound to create effects, e.g. onomatopoeia.**   3.3 T15

Word and sentence level objective

- To collect synonyms which will be useful in writing poems.   3.3 W13

LESSON ONE

MODEL TEXT

- Start the lesson by asking children what sounds they hear in the morning. Make a list, e.g. *alarm clock* <u>ringing</u>, *birds* <u>singing</u>. Ask them if they know the name for the underlined words.

- Write the word *onomatopoeia* on a flipchart and read it aloud slowly. Can the pupils come up with a simple definition?

- Explain the lesson objective: *to look at a poem that uses onomatopoeia.*

- Read aloud the first verse of *The Sound Collector*. Ask children to anticipate what sounds might have been 'carried away'.

- Ask different groups to join in with the next five verses. Read the last verse yourself. Discuss why 'life will never be the same'.

- Ask pupils if they can spot any examples of onomatopoeia in verse 2? *purring, ticking, whistling*

- Look at verse 4. What made a *ticking* sound? *grill*

- Can pupils think of a good way to read *hissing* aloud?

- What word imitates the noise of a curtain? *swishing*

- Which words in each verse rhyme? *lines 2 and 4*

Word and sentence level work

1 Listen to the sounds you hear in the classroom. Ask pupils to suggest words to describe these. They should invent words if necessary.

2 Ask pupils to think of some 'sound' words to describe water falling, e.g drip, splash, trickle. Pupils should then use a thesaurus to look up synonyms for each one. Which are onomatopoeic? Make a list.

Group activities: differentiation

Pupils work in mixed ability groups using **PCM 71**. Half the class should prepare to read aloud verses 1, 2 and 3; the other half verses 4, 5 and 6. They can all read the last verse in the plenary.

Plenary

Listen to verses 1 to 3. Pupils comment on the effects created by the way the sound words were read. Then listen to verses 4 to 6. Read the last verse together.

YOU WILL NEED

- Flipchart
- **OHT 36** – The Sound Collector
- **PCM 71** – The Sound Collector
- **PCM 72** – Homework

ICT For activities linked to this lesson see **PAGE 108**

HOMEWORK

Pupils use **PCM 72** to record the things they hear after the end of school, and think of onomatopoeic words to describe the sound.

Link to reading objective

- To select, prepare, read aloud and recite by heart, poems that play with language; to recognise patterns of sound that create effects.　　3.3 T7

Assumed prior knowledge

- Choose and prepare poems for performance.　　3.2 T4
- Collect suitable words for poems.　　3.1 T13
- Synonyms.　　3.1 W18

Planning suggestion

You may follow this unit with group readings of the poems pupils have written. Pupils can then browse and collect more examples of poems which use onomatopoeia.

LESSON TWO

SHARED WRITING

- Share some of the things pupils recorded for homework and the words they used to imitate the sounds.

- Explain the lesson objective: *to start to write a poem using some of their onomatopoeic words.*

- Read aloud 'Morning' by Grace Nichols. Ask pupils to identify the sounds the poet hears in the morning. What onomatopoeic words does she use to describe them? e.g. *clinking, popping, singing*

- Which words are repeated in every line? *Morning comes*

- Refer briefly to the last line, and suggest that the poet sees morning as a bossy kind of person, in charge of the day.

- Now tell pupils that as they collected their sounds in the afternoon, their poem will be called 'Afternoon'.

- Using pupils' suggestions, begin to write an 'Afternoon' poem. Write two or three lines together. Use -ing endings.

- Tell pupils that they can write their own lines to end the poem.

Group activities and differentiation

All pupils use their homework ideas and those from shared writing to write their own 'Afternoon' poem, using **PCM 73** for support if necessary. **Lower attainers** can use the lines from shared writing to start them off and write two or three more lines of their own.

Guided writing. Support **lower attainers** in using onomatopoeic words. Help **higher attainers** to think of ideas for the last line. What sort of person can they link Afternoon to?

Plenary

Organise a readers' circle, with pupils following each other in reading their own lines. Comment on onomatopoeic words, especially any they have invented. Talk about pupils' final lines and make a list of similes and metaphors to describe afternoon.

EXTENDED WRITING

Pupils finish writing their 'Afternoon' poems, then read them through with a partner and make any changes. They then make a final illustrated copy for a class book.

YOU WILL NEED

- **Pupil's Book** page 66
- **OHT 37** – Afternoon writing frame
- **PCM 73** – Afternoon writing frame

ICT For activities linked to this lesson see **PAGE 108**

WATCH OUT FOR

- ▶ Extra detail which stops the flow of the poem.
- ▶ Misunderstanding of onomatopoeic words.

A to Z Book • ALPHABETICAL TEXTS

MAIN WRITING OBJECTIVES

- **To make alphabetically ordered texts, using information from other subjects or information books.**   3.3.T24
- **To use IT to bring to a published form.**   3.3 T21

Word and sentence level objectives

- To become aware of the use of commas in marking grammatical boundaries.   3.3 S7

LESSON ONE

MODEL TEXT

- Explain the lesson objective: *to look at an alphabetical text.*
- Can pupils think of any examples of alphabetical texts that they use? *dictionary, thesaurus, encyclopedia, indexes etc*
- Why is it useful to present information in this way?
- Read aloud the report about a North American Indian camp. Jade wrote this as part of a project on North American Indians. She then presented her information as an alphabetical reference text. Look at the first few entries in her A to Z book.
- Discuss how the A to Z book is set out. *using headings in alphabetical order*
- Look at Jade's report on the OHT and ask pupils to identify the key words she has used as headings in her A to Z Book. Why do you think she has chosen them? *they are about the most important things*
- Look at the entry for **Animals**. What information from the report is left out of the entry? *details about what the individual animals were used for*
- Point out that the entries are short and focus on the key facts.
- Ask pupils to suggest what the words in brackets tell you.

Word and sentence level work

Look at Jade's report and ask pupils to identify where commas are used to mark pauses in sentences, and to separate lists, e.g. *buffalo, deer, elk, horses and dogs*

Group activities: differentiation

Pupils work in pairs to read through Jade's report on **PCM 74** and identify other key words that could be used as headings. They write them out in alphabetical order.
Higher attainers can begin to draft a short entry for the first heading.

Plenary

Look at the key words pupils have chosen. Are they appropriate? Ask some pupils to read their entries. Are they short enough? Do they include key facts only?

YOU WILL NEED

- **Pupil's Book** page 68
- **OHT 38** – North American Indians
- **PCM 74** – North American Indians

 ICT For activities linked to this lesson see **PAGE 108**

HOMEWORK

Discuss work in another subject, or a class topic that pupils have been working on. Ask them to make notes for an A to Z book. What are the key areas of information? What headings could they use?

Link to reading objectives

- To scan alphabetically ordered texts to locate information quickly. 3.3 T17
- To summarise the content of text orally. 3.3 T19

Assumed prior knowledge

- Alphabetically ordered texts. 2.2
- Simple non-chronological reports. 3.1 T23
- Recording information; notes and key words. 3.2 T17

Planning suggestion

This unit can be used to support work in other subjects or on a class topic. Pupils can reinforce their skills in using alphabetically ordered texts to find information, before putting together a text of their own.

LESSON TWO

SHARED WRITING

- Recap the key features of alphabetical reference books.

- Explain the lesson objective: *to create an A to Z Book about a class topic.*

- Introduce the topic. Ask pupils to contribute ideas for entries and jot them down on the flipchart. Use examples of pupils' topic/subject writing to find more ideas. Demonstrate how to use the index from a library book on the topic to suggest other ideas.

- Ask pupils to pick out words you could use as headings in an A to Z Book. Which one comes first alphabetically? Adapt the writing frame if you need to, but it would be good to start with 'A'.

- Model writing the entry, helping pupils to edit out information which isn't necessary, and to keep the entry short.

- Write one or two more entries with pupils, reminding them to pick headings in alphabetical order. Use 'see below' (or 'above') if a key word is going to be explained elsewhere.

- Allocate a letter of the alphabet to each pair and leave the list of headings clearly displayed. Higher attaining pairs can be given more than one letter.

Group activities: differentiation

Pupils work in pairs to identify headings and compile entries for the class A to Z book. They should read it through to check that it is short and clear. **Higher attainers** can write more than one entry for their letter.

Guided writing. Help pupils to edit their entries and to think about key words they have used which other pairs will be writing about. Add in cross-references where appropriate.

Plenary

Check on progress so far. Do the entries give enough information? Or too much? Has anything important been missed out as a heading?

EXTENDED WRITING

Pupils continue to compile entries for the A to Z book. You could do a shared session to edit the book for clarity and to remove any unnecessary duplication. Publish the final version using ICT.

YOU WILL NEED

- **OHT 39** – A–Z book writing frame
- Flipchart

OHT 39

ICT For activities linked to this lesson see PAGE 108

 WATCH OUT FOR
▶ Over-long entries.
▶ Vague entries.

What makes a good writer?

● PROGRESS REVIEW

MAIN WRITING OBJECTIVES

- To review progress over the year/term in meeting the NLS objectives.
- To develop an understanding of what makes a good writer.

LESSON ONE

YOU WILL NEED

- **Pupil's Book** page 70
- **PCM 75** – Statements
- **PCM 76** – Homework

MODEL TEXT

- Explain the lesson objective: *to discuss what makes a good writer.*

- Ask pupils to summarise what they think makes a good writer. Talk briefly about the written work they have done this year. What kinds of writing have they really enjoyed? What do they think they've learned to do well? What things have they found hard to write?

- Explain that one Year 3 class filled in a questionnaire about writing.

- Read 'What Makes a Good Writer' aloud.

- Explore some of the ideas. What is meant by 'uses own life and imagination'? *use things that you know about and that mean something to you, as well as making things up* Refer back to the Jamila Gavin interview in Unit 1.

- Discuss why it is important to think about who your writing is for. *so you know how to write, what words to use, what you need to say*

- Continue the discussion by comparing the responses on the questionnaire with pupils' own ideas. Share your own views and experiences as a writer.

- Discuss solutions for some of the things that are hard, e.g. how reading lots of different stories can help you with ideas for endings, how working together can help you get going, how practise can help with letter writing.

Group activities: differentiation

Working in groups or pairs, pupils discuss the statements on **PCM 75** and decide whether they agree or disagree.

Guided reading. Discuss the statements with pupils and the reasons for agreement or disagreement.

Plenary

Look at each of the statements and take a vote about whether pupils agree or disagree. Does everyone feel the same? Discuss some of the most contentious statements.

ICT For activities linked to this lesson see **PAGE 108**

HOMEWORK

Pupils answer the writing questionnaire on **PCM 76**.

Link to reading objective

- To refer to significant aspects of the text and to know how language is used to create these.

3.3 T2

Assumed prior knowledge

- Coverage of the full range of Year 3 writing objectives and text types, and knowledge of appropriate terminology.

Planning suggestion

This unit could be worked on towards the end of the year as part of pupils' self-assessment.

LESSON TWO

SHARED WRITING

- Discuss any new thoughts arising from the homework.

- With pupils, look back on the different kinds of writing they have done in school this year.

- Ask pupils to think about any writing they have done outside school – stories, lists, letters, diaries, notes etc. Discuss the different reasons there are for writing things down. Who do you write for?

- After a short discussion, begin to classify the writing into different text types. Ask pupils to think of specific examples of writing they have done under each text type, and add a blob to the appropriate part of chart. Which leg has most blobs? Which has least?

- Discuss the sentence starters at the bottom. What do children feel they have achieved this year? What sort of targets might they set for next year?

- If pupils suggest 'improve spelling and handwriting' as their main target, explain that it is more important to have good ideas and to think about the content and organisation of the writing. Spellings can always be checked before you write out a final version.

Group activities: differentiation

Working individually, pupils fill in a personal spider chart, using **PCM 77**. They can discuss their work with a partner to help them remember all the things they have done during the year. They then set themselves targets for next year. **Lower attainers** could answer the questions orally.

Guided writing. Help pupils to set themselves targets by looking at the things they find hard to do.

Plenary

What are the areas where children have made most progress? Are there any common targets? Discuss how you might plan to achieve them.

EXTENDED WRITING

Pupils can produce a final copy of their progress review, together with targets for next year. Add it to pupils' records of achievement or other assessment documents.

YOU WILL NEED
- **OHT 40** – Spider Chart
- **PCM 77** – Spider Chart

ICT For activities linked to this lesson see **PAGE 108**

WATCH OUT FOR
▶ Difficulty in distinguishing different text types.
▶ Fixation with spelling.

Information and Communication Technology

ICT and its place in the UK Curriculum

The curricula for England, Wales, Scotland and Northern Ireland all require that ICT should be used to support writing and learning about language. The Literacy Hour is an ideal starting place for many of these activities. By incorporating ICT activities into the Literacy Hour and other writing sessions, many elements of the ICT Programmes of Study may be taught in 'real' contexts.

The National Curriculum Orders for England & Wales, the 5–14 Guidelines for Scotland and the Education Technology Strategy 1996–2000 in Northern Ireland, all give ICT a prominent place across all curriculum areas and give an entitlement for all pupils to achieve ICT capability.

ICT and Literacy

Literacy in the 21st century involves making sense of language and writing in many different contexts. In responding to texts, children must learn to recognise and be critical of the rich range of media; in producing their own writing, they must learn to use different media appropriately to suit their audience and purpose.

Children should be encouraged to explore the extent to which page-layout and design, use of colour, choice of fonts and text styles can enhance their writing. They also have opportunities, through the world wide web and multimedia authoring, to publish for wider audiences and to communicate via e-mail with children throughout the world.

During the Literacy Hour, pupils may be using ICT to support language and literacy development as well as developing their personal ICT capability.

Opportunities to develop the ICT skills associated with these activities can be included in the Literacy Hour and at other times throughout the week. The suggested activities provided in *Models for Writing* offer some starting points.

ICT to support whole class and group work

ICT can support and enhance discursive and interactive whole-class teaching and group work. The range of software available varies from fairly straightforward presentation packages available with standard office-type applications to fully-featured multimedia authoring tools. Interactive whiteboards, wide-format monitors, an LCD tablet with high-powered OHP, daylight projectors or large TV monitors should all be considered as options for presenting to groups. These vary considerably in price and are likely to represent significant capital investments for many primary schools. Teachers should discuss the options available with the ICT Co-ordinator or local advisory service.

When planning to use presentation software, consider what the 'added value' will be to pupils over traditional methods such as big books, flip-charts, blackboard and chalk, video, TV, radio, OHT, whiteboard and marker pen. A major advantage is that your presentation is stored in digital form and may be re-used for other purposes. If your presentation includes input from children during the session, this will also be stored for future use. Furthermore, a multimedia presentation allows a range of media to be used from one single workstation rather than juggling between an OHP, video and big book.

Models for Writing is accompanied by a set of colour OHTs which are an integral part of shared reading and writing. The OHTs contain extracts from model texts, and provide a wide variety of writing and planning frames to support pupils in developing their reading and writing skills. They allow the teacher to model both the reading and the writing processes to the class, and OHT pens can be used to highlight teaching points.

Audio-recording equipment is another valuable ICT tool. For example, when discussing performance poetry it may be used to enable children to experiment with different styles of delivery, evaluating each others' recordings.

Alternative input devices such as overlay keyboards, onscreen grids, touchscreens and voice input may be particularly useful to support young children who are not fully conversant with the QWERTY keyboard, or who need 'whole word' support for writing activities.

ICT for writing, editing and publishing

Using ICT to support children's writing means far more than simply asking them to word-process their text. The use of ICT can help children compose, transform and present text, and will give them a growing understanding and confidence in literacy, language, layout, style and design. Whether the writing and presentation of a text involves illustrating a poem, setting out information in a chart, or annotating a diagram, ICT can be used to support the activity and examples are provided in *Models for Writing*.

When writing, the children can change their work using various tools. Cutting and pasting paragraphs, sentences and words gives children the freedom to experiment with their text and decide the most appropriate way of ordering it. Using the electronic thesaurus allows the children to expand their vocabulary, and the spell-checker gives them the opportunity to check and correct their work. The final piece of writing will have a high standard of presentation that has been developed and adapted to suit the audience and the purpose of the piece.

As far as you are able, it is important to choose appropriate software for these activities. Some word-processing packages are capable of handling text and images to produce more sophisticated work, but if you want the children to begin to learn transferable skills associated with desktop publishing (DTP) you will achieve far better results with a desktop publishing program than with a word-processor.

Teachers who are confident with computers, and who have the appropriate painting or drawing software can also consider the use of ICT to illustrate children's work, where such an activity supports the learning objective.

Writing and the Internet

The Internet provides many opportunities for developing communication skills. Children should think about the emerging styles of writing which are appropriate for e-mail messages and be given opportunities to send and receive e-mail for real purposes. They may have 'net-pals' who will be interested in some of the writing arising from the activities in *Models for Writing*. Some of the activities lend themselves to setting up an e-mail project between schools in the UK using this scheme, or using a unit in the scheme as the starting point for a project with schools in other parts of the world.

Preparing some writing for the school website is another means whereby children will be writing for real and wider unknown audiences. There are two ways in which pupils may 'publish' on the web. They may have produced some writing for print which may be 'showcased' in a gallery on the school website. There may also be opportunities for children to design part of the school website or even their own website.

ICT and *Models for Writing*

On pages 102–108 you will find ICT activities for each unit of *Models for Writing*.

On pages 109–112 you will find a **Glossary of ICT terms**. This explains the ICT terminology used in the activities and gives simple, practical examples of what the terminology means.

Preparation and organisation of activities

In preparing to use ICT with *Models for Writing* teachers should check with the ICT Co-ordinator what hardware and software are available for use with Year 3. It is important to plan the development of ICT resources in consultation with other teachers, the Literacy Co-ordinator and ICT Co-ordinator. Many of the activities and resources prepared for use in one year group may be quickly modified for use by colleagues in other year groups if there is a school-wide policy on how to create and store digital material.

The ICT Co-ordinator will be able to advise on the most appropriate software to use for different applications, in particular when graphics are being created and stored.

Another important co-ordination function is to ensure that children have had the opportunity to learn the basic ICT skills they will need to use in order to carry out some of the activities suggested in *Models for Writing*.

The time taken to prepare the ICT activities for *Models for Writing* will depend on the ICT competence and confidence of teachers, as well as the software and hardware available in school. It may be appropriate for non-teaching assistants to do some of the preparatory tasks under the direction of a Year 3 teacher. Once the basic preparation is done, the resources will be available to, and may be modified and adapted for each class.

It is important to plan how to develop, save and back-up all ICT resources using a systematic and agreed filing structure either on floppy disks, CD-ROM or a school network. Discuss the systems with the ICT Co-ordinator and develop a whole-school approach to managing digital resources.

IMPORTANT NOTE:

Several of the following ICT activities instruct you to prepare a text-file of the model text.

It is important to be aware that the keying in and electronic storage of copyright material is a breach of copyright law. The Publisher has obtained permission for the classroom activitites suggested in *Models for Writing*, but the keyed texts should not be stored on a network or otherwise transferred electronically.

If in doubt, consult your Copyright and Licensing Authority document.

Models for Writing: ICT activities

(Please note that these do not include the use of OHTs, which are within the main lesson plans for each unit.)

UNIT	TITLE	LESSON ONE	LESSON TWO
1	Talking to Jamila Gavin	Demonstrate how the use of 'outline' view in a word-processor provides useful support for drafting ideas and organising the structure for a story.	Compare this use of ICT with the star chart suggested by Jamila Gavin. Prepare sample fiction texts and **word-banks** using 'outline' view. Each sample text should include the story idea and headings for all the key elements. Pupils work in pairs or small groups to gather material and start to plan a story using the sample text.
2	Familiar Places	Prepare a **word-bank** including introductory settings, phrases, and words linked with the playground, playtime and lunchtime. This will provide pupils with support for writing and revising their description of the playground. Using the **word-bank**, pupils work in pairs to write descriptions of the playground.	Use a **thesaurus** to explore a range of synonyms to make the setting more interesting.
3	Cat Speak	Prepare a **template** in a word-processing package with headings for the Report Planner.	Using the Report Planner template, pupils work in pairs to write a non-chronological report.
4	Harry's Party	Prepare a **text file** of the model texts with a **word-bank** including features of dialogue and alternatives for 'said'.	Demonstrate how to use the <shift> key for capital letters, question marks and speech marks. Pupils use the **word-bank** to write their copy to include speech marks and other features of dialogue.
5	Ace Dragon Ltd	Prepare a **text file** of the model text and a **word-bank** for stage directions. Using a talking word-processor, pupils will gain sound and text support. Demonstrate how to use the <shift> key for an exclamation mark.	Prepare a template or stylesheet for playscript layout in a word-processor or desktop publishing (DTP) package. Pupils use the template and **text file** to re-write the model text as a playscript, concentrating on accurate punctuation. Pupils proof-read each others' work and make corrections. Save and print out a copy for each member of the cast to read from. Discuss the advantages of using a word-processor for re-drafting and making multiple copies of playscripts.

UNIT	TITLE	LESSON ONE	LESSON TWO
6	People and Places	Using a **graphics package**, pupils illustrate the verbs identified in the model text.	Prepare a **word-bank** for a place or person known well by everyone in the class. Using 'outline' view in a word-processor or planning software with the **word-bank**, pupils work in pairs to write a joint report.
7	Rhythm Machine	Use a variety of fonts and shapes containing text to form different types of shape poems including calligrams. Demonstrate how to achieve these effects to the class. NB. This activity should be done using a drawing or painting package rather than a word-processor.	Pupils explore the use of colour, pattern, fonts, shapes of letters and words to create shape poems and calligrams. Save and print these for display. Discuss how using ICT is different from stencils, paint, crayons and pencils for creating these effects.
8	Frogs and Toads	Extend the 'Spot the Difference' discussion into an introduction to **databases**.	Prepare a set of blank record cards using the headings (fields) to describe frogs and toads. Show how these cards may be used to describe other animals and introduce the idea of 'records'. Collect data about a topic currently being studied and present it on numbered record cards. Ask the class to sort the record cards, using the fields to answer simple questions.
9	Like and Hate	Prepare a **text file** of the model texts and a **word-bank**. Using the model text: *Tomato 1*, pupils re-write the poem as prose to include speech marks. Demonstrate how to use the \<shift\> key for speech marks.	Use the thesaurus in the word-processor to select alternatives for the verbs. Replace some of the verbs with synonyms, save and print these and read the new poems to the class. Discuss the advantages and limitations of a thesaurus.

UNIT	TITLE	LESSON ONE	LESSON TWO
10	Once Upon a Time ... the End	Prepare a **text file** and **word-bank** of the model texts. Using a talking word-processor, pupils will gain sound and text support to write their own story beginnings, based on one of the extracts.	Demonstrate using **cut**, **paste** and **copy**. Pupils continue to write the story making use of paragraphs, gaining support from the **word-bank**. Discuss the advantages of using a word-processor to plan, draft and revise stories.
11	Who? What? Where?	Invite a writer who uses ICT to plan his or her stories into school to talk with the children about how ICT is useful and when other methods are more appropriate.	
12	A Poor Widow's Son	Prepare **templates** in a desktop publishing (DTP) package with image boxes and text frames for a Wanted or Missing Person poster.	Pupils use the template to create their own posters for the Goodies and Baddies gallery. Using a graphics package, pupils illustrate their posters to match the written description. Save and print the posters.
13	Memo to me	Demonstrate how the use of 'outline' view in a word-processor or other planning software application provides useful support for making notes. Demonstrate how to mark and delete or cut and paste words to organise the notes and plan sentences. Compare this use of ICT with other methods for making notes: post-its, memo slips, scraps of paper etc.	Using 'outline' view, pupils work in pairs to expand the notes to write character descriptions of class members. Save and print the descriptions. This could be built into a 'guess who?' game for use in PSHE.
14	Jack's Journey	Let the children explore a CD adventure game which uses a map interface. Discuss how this differs from using paper-based maps with stories.	Discuss the strengths of each in terms of helping our understanding and enjoyment of the story. Prepare a template in a graphics or desktop publishing (DTP) package based on a map of the area around the school. Using the template, their own artwork, clipart or images taken with a digital camera, the pupils illustrate a journey and use it to re-tell a story.

UNIT	TITLE	LESSON ONE	LESSON TWO
15	Hamsters must not …	Prepare sample texts of familiar rules and associated **word-banks**.	Demonstrate how to achieve different styles for lists in a word-processor: bulletted lists, numbered lists, font size, upper/lower case, centred text, bold text, colour. Pupils experiment with styles for the sets of rules depending on how they will be displayed. Pupils should save and print each layout as a basis for group or class discussion about appropriate use of styles.
16	Too Much Searching	Prepare a story chain using 'outline' view.	Compare this use of ICT with the Story Chain on **OHT 22**. Using 'outline' view in a word-processor, work in pairs to expand the notes to write a cumulative story chain.
17	Mighty Mountain	Prepare a grid template in a desktop publishing (DTP) package with image boxes and text frames. Using a graphics package, pupils illustrate the opposites.	Pupils use the template to create illustrated pairs of opposites which may be printed, stuck onto card and made into a matching game.
18	How to …	Prepare sample texts and **word-banks** for sets of instructions which the alien will need to be familiar with. Prepare templates in a desktop publishing (DTP) package with image boxes and text frames for sets of instructions.	Pupils use the templates, sample texts and **word-banks** to create sets of instructions for the alien. Using a graphics package, pupils illustrate their instructions. Save and print the instructions and make them into a manual for the alien.

UNIT	TITLE	LESSON ONE	LESSON TWO
19	Getting to the Point	Prepare sample texts of some non-fiction passages from a CD or website, referencing sources. Demonstrate how to use the highlighter function (or other style if this is not available) in a word-processor to pick out key words and phrases. Demonstate how to select and delete text.	Using a talking word-processor, pupils highlight key words and phrases. Deleting other text leaves pupils with 'notes' on which to base their own writing. Compare this method of making notes (when using text already in a digital form) with other methods. Introduce issues about copyright and referencing sources in a discussion.
20	The Hairy Toe	Using simple musical composition software, pupils experiment with sound samples and record these as sound effects for the poetry reading.	Prepare the model text in a desktop publishing (DTP) or presentation package. Using a graphics package, pupils illustrate the poem and add the sound samples. Present the poetry reading to the class.
21	Sea World	Prepare sample texts of the model texts.	Demonstrate the **word-count** function. Using a talking word-processor, pupils highlight key words and phrases. Summarise the text for each paragraph. Use the word-count function to cut the summary down to 50 words.
22	The Market Street Mystery	Prepare sample texts of the model texts. Show pupils where the apostrophe key is on the keyboard. Pupils contract words in the letter, using the apostrophe, highlighting each one.	Save and print the revised letter. Discuss how contracting the words changes the tone of the letter. Ask how many children have access to **e-mail**. Discuss how children might communicate with each other about this event using **e-mail**, a very informal style for recounting events.
23	Diary of a Killer Cat	Prepare sample texts of the model texts. Using the sample text, pupils may either replace all pronouns with nouns or re-write the story in the third person.	Save and print the new stories and read them aloud. Discuss what effect the changes have. Using the sample text, pupils write new entries for Jake's diary.

UNIT	TITLE	LESSON ONE	LESSON TWO
24	May We Recommend	Use the Review Frames as the basis for discussing building a **database** for book reviews. Prepare a set of blank record cards using the headings (fields) in the fiction and non-fiction review frames. Show how these cards may be used to record book reviews and introduce the idea of 'records'. Introduce the idea of keywords for each 'free text' field and discuss the importance of accurate spelling (demonstrate results from a simple search using correct and incorrect spellings).	Prepare a simple **database** with an appropriate field structure to include books commonly read by Year 3. Use this as a Year group resource to summarise, share, catalogue and interrogate information about books read in Year 3.
25	Dear Author	Go to http://www.nawe.co.uk and invite a poet to come into school or discuss their ideas by **e-mail**.	E-mail links with another school, or author who uses e-mail, would provide children with first-hand examples of using e-mail for sharing ideas about books they have read. There are many sites which offer 'partner-finding' services. Try the partner-finding area of the European Schoolnet website at http://www.en.eun.org/ menu/projects/partners.html or set up a local project in the LEA with other schools using *Models for Writing*.
26	Flood! 1	Prepare a **word-bank** of words and phrases showing the passage of time. Demonstrate how the use of 'outline' view in a word-processor or other planning software application provides useful support for planning stories and finding the 'natural' breaks for paragraphs and chapters which signal the sequence of time or change of place for the story.	Using 'outline' view in a word-processor or planning software and the **word-bank**, pupils work in the pairs to plan their own chapter stories, thinking carefully about chapter headings. Emphasise that, at this stage in extended writing, the focus is on planning, rather than writing 'polished' sentences, and using styles to present their work. This will be done in Unit 27.

UNIT	TITLE	LESSON ONE	LESSON TWO
27	Flood! 2	Prepare a set of **stylesheets** in a desk-top publishing (DTP) package to incorporate chapters and paragraph styles. Demonstrate how to use the \<shift\> key for speech marks and \<return\> key for a new paragraph. Pupils write, redraft and revise their chapters, working individually and in pairs using a talking word-processor with word-bank and spell-checker.	Pupils develop the plans from Unit 26 and import text and images (created from original artwork or clip-art collection) into the stylesheets. Pupils edit, re-draft and revise their stories to create interesting dialogue, correctly punctuated and laid up.
28	The Sound Collector	Using simple musical composition software, audio recorders and microphones, pupils experiment with sound samples and record these as sound effects for the Afternoon poem. Pupils write their poems and, using a graphics package, illustrate the poem and add the sound samples.	Present the Afternoon poem to the class.
29	A to Z Book	Prepare a simple **database** with an appropriate record and field structure to support a topic being studied by the class.	Introduce the idea of keywords and discuss the importance of accurate spelling (demonstrate results from a simple search using correct and incorrect spellings). Pupils contribute to the **database** using their research from books, CDs and other resources.
30	What makes a good writer?	Prepare a presentation of the range of ICT applications children have used throughout the year to support writing: word-banks, templates, stylesheets, e-mail, databases, music software, DTP, word-processing and graphics packages. Incorporate a selection of work produced by members of the class during the Year, showing developing expertise.	Discuss which ICT skills and techniques they have learned. Ask the children to identify some of the different uses they make of ICT at school and home.

Glossary of ICT terms

All teachers will need to understand and use the vocabulary associated with ICT and help children to use it appropriately and in context.

This list provides a broad summary of terms and acronyms which will be needed to provide support for children at Key Stage 2.

Address: the unique identifier for a web page. Typically an address takes the form http://www.repp.co.uk and should be entered into the address bar on the browser window. In this example, <repp.> is the name of the company owning the website, <co.> indicates that it is a company (others include <org.> for organisation, <gov.> for government, <sch.> for school, <ac.>for university etc.) and <uk> indicates the country. No country code usually indicates a US based website or a site, which regards itself as international.

Application: a piece of software, usually installed onto the computer or run over a network.

Attachment (see enclosure): a file sent with an e-mail message. An attachment may be text, graphics or sound. It may be helpful to imagine them as 'paper-clipped' to a file as a note may be attached to a paper document.

Authoring software (see presentation software): an application which enables the user to create documents using mixed media including text, still and moving images, and sound, with a means of moving between pages or screens. These packages may be used to produce presentations for use in the classroom or hall, as well as for creating web pages.

Back up: to make copies of documents or applications on another disk or tape as a safeguard against data loss. It is essential to keep regular back ups. Check the school policy with the ICT Co-ordinator.

Bookmark (see favourite): to store the address of a web page in a list in order to return to it during another session browsing the world wide web.

Browse: to move from page to page on a website or CD-ROM.

Browser software: an application which displays the pages of a website. The two major browser applications are Microsoft *Internet Explorer* and *Netscape Navigator*.

Clip art: images available commercially or as free collections distributed on disks, CD-ROM or the Internet, which may be incorporated into documents, multimedia presentations and websites.

Cut and paste: to move text or images from a document and place them in another part of the same document or into another document.

Database software: an application which enables the user to set up fields and records containing data, and to sort the data and display the information in a number of ways including graphs and charts.

Daylight projector: a piece of equipment which projects the display from a computer onto an external screen. The projectors may be wall- or ceiling-mounted or stand-alone portable devices.

DTP (desktop publishing) software: an application which enables the user to combine text and graphics, using templates for page-layout and styles. Text and graphics are typically placed in text or picture frames after having been originally created in word-processing, text-editing, painting or drawing packages.

Digital: information which is held in numerical form. Typically, in a computer, this is as a sequence of binary numbers.

Directory: a folder on the desktop which contains documents and sub-directories enabling users to organise their work, and find documents and applications easily. The directory system is often likened to a filing cabinet, with drawers, sub-divisions and folders.

Document: a single piece of work. A document may be in a word-processor, desktop publisher or database application. Each document must be saved with a unique filename.

Download: to save material such as text, images or software from another computer, the Internet or a network, and store it locally for future use on a hard disk or school network.

E-mail (electronic mail): a service provided on the Internet whereby electronic messages may be sent by one user to one or many other users throughout the world in a few minutes at minimal cost. In order to use e-mail, users will need to have e-mail software and a profile set up which includes a personal e-mail address.

Enclosure (see attachment): a file sent with an e-mail message. An enclosure may be text, graphics or sound.

Favourite (sometimes spelled favorite, see bookmark): to store the address of a web page in a list in order to return to it during another session browsing the world wide web.

Filename: the name used when saving a document as a file. It is important to use filenames that you and others will understand when sharing documents on a network or creating collections of digital resources.

Font: a set of type characters in the same style. A font will include different weights (bold, light, book) and different slants (italic, oblique). There are numerous fonts, some will be supplied with each application, others may be purchased or obtained from free collections.

Graphic: an image or picture.

Hyperlink: the electronic link to related information (text, graphics, sound, entire documents, whole pages or websites) which enables users to browse the Internet or a CD-ROM by making their own choices about routes through the material. The cursor will usually change from an arrow to, for example, a hand icon when it is over a hyperlink. Hyperlinks are often highlighted in some way such as underlining. Clicking on a hyperlink takes the user to the related page or website.

Image box (or image frame): the placeholder for a graphic, picture or image in a document.

Interactive whiteboard: a large, touch-sensitive board onto which an image of the computer desktop is projected. Users can interact with the projected image by drawing on the board with a stylus.

ISP (Internet service provider): the company providing Internet services such as e-mail and access to the world wide web for a school, organisation, business or household. Some ISPs do not charge for their services but may carry advertising. Check with your ICT Co-ordinator how to access Internet services from school.

Internet: the network of networks. Networks are formed by connecting computers. The Internet has been formed by connecting networks into a global network of networks. It provides a set of protocols which allow different networks to talk to each other, and services such as e-mail and the world wide web.

Intranet: a closed, private network or network of networks which uses the same protocols as the Internet and provides the same services such as e-mail.

LCD (liquid crystal display) panel: a flat screen display which can be used with a high powered overhead projector for presentations to groups.

Multimedia: the presentation of information through the use of more than one medium e.g. text, sound, images.

Network: formed by connecting computers in order to share files and applications. Networks are either peer-to-peer where any computer can talk to any other computer on the network or client/server where one computer holds all the files and applications and can be accessed by the client computers.

Optical character recognition (OCR) software: an application which enables a scanner to 'read' text and convert it into a digital form. Once saved, the text may be exported to a word-processor for editing.

PDF (portable document format): a proprietary document file format, for which a reader is freely available from Adobe, which has been designed to ensure that documents, particularly DTP documents retain all their formatting and typographic styles and effects when viewed on another computer.

Presentation software (see authoring software): an application which enables the user to create documents using mixed media including text, still and moving images and sound with a means of moving between pages or screens. These packages may be used to produce presentations for use in the classroom or hall.

Scanner: a piece of equipment which enables users to copy paper-based materials such as photographs or illustrations and save them in digital format. A scanner produces a bitmap image composed of pixels and works in a similar way to a photocopier. Many scanners include OCR software as standard.

Search engine: a service provided commercially on the Internet used to search for documents on the Internet. Users access the search engine from a web page on the providers website by entering key words. The service is usually free to the user and paid for by advertising.

Spell-checker: a function available in most word-processors and many other software applications which enables users to check spelling. It is important to remember that spell-checkers use a dictionary stored on the computer and will search it for logical matches. Users will need a certain basic level of spelling strategies to be able to make use of this facility. A spell-checker will not pick up mis-spelt words that are in the wrong context (for example, 'there' and 'their'). Some software has grammar checkers which teachers should consider using with care. Check what conventions are used. The problem with many grammar and spell-checker software is that is uses US English, although there may be opportunities to customise the dictionaries.

Stylesheet (see also template): 'blank' documents which may be saved to include margins, text styles, headers, footers, page-numbering, guidelines, image frames and text boxes amongst many other features which may be set up so that every page has a common format.

Table: a function available in some word-processors and spreadsheets to organise lists into tables. These may then be sorted according to various criteria such as date, alphabetical order, number etc. Tables should be used in preference to the <tab> key when putting lists into a word-processor.

Talking word-processor: speech output is available in some word-processing packages. The user may hear individual letters, words or complete sentences as they are keyed in, or on demand. This is very valuable as support for reading and writing activities.

Template: 'blank' documents which may be saved to include margins, text styles, headers, footers, page-numbering, guidelines, image frames and text boxes amongst many other features which may be set up so that every page has a common format. They are essential for use in desktop publishing packages and useful for word-processing. When writing more than a short paragraph, it is 'good practice' to set up styles for the entire document rather than make 'local' changes to, for example, centre and embolden a heading.

Text file: any file which contains plain text. When transferring text between different applications and computer platforms, it is advisable to select rich text format (RTF) from the save options.

Text frame (text box): the placeholder for text in a desktop publishing document.

Thesaurus: a function available in many word-processing applications for finding a synonym, an antonym, or related words for a selected word in the user's text.

Typing tutor: an application which trains users to touch type, typically using a structured 'drill' approach with on-screen copy to practise typing from.

Undo: a useful feature available in most software applications. Reverses the last action and may be used more than once in some applications to retrace a series of actions.

Website: a collection of pages published on the world wide web.

Word count: a function available in many word-processing applications for automatically counting the number of words, pages, characters and lines in a selected part of the document or the entire document.

Word-bank: a collection of words, customised by the user and stored in a word-processor. Many word-processors designed for the education market have word-bank facilities whereby selected groups of words and phrases may be saved and used to support writing. Check with the documentation in the program available for how to create and save word-banks.

Word-processing software: an application which enables users to manipulate text.

World wide web: an Internet service which provides information in the form of pages which can include text, images, video clips and sound. These are viewed using a web browser.